THE TENTH MAN

*The Tenth Man is the only Man.
There is No Other.*

十僧頓悟

The
Tenth Man

THE GREAT JOKE

(which made Lazarus laugh)

Wei Wu Wei

SENTIENT PUBLICATIONS, LLC

Cover design by Kim Johansen, Black Dog Design

Library of Congress Cataloging-in-Publication Data

Wei, Wu Wei.
  The tenth man the great joke (which made Lazarus laugh) / Wei
Wu Wei.—1st Sentient Publications ed.
      p. cm.
  Includes index.
  ISBN 1-59181-007-8
  1. Asia—Religion. 2. Philosophy, Asian. 3. Buddhism—Doctrines.
4. Taoism—Doctrines. I. Title.

BL1023.W45 2003
291.2'2—cd21

                                                    2002042947

SENTIENT PUBLICATIONS

A Limited Liability Company
1113 Spruce Street
Boulder, CO 80302
www.sentientpublications.com

Foreword to the Second Edition

BY PROFESSION, I am a licensed clinical psychologist. I was in private practice for thirty-seven years, and my work as a psychotherapist was fairly traditional. I was always drawn to Eastern religions and philosophies and most of my private studies were in this area. I viewed myself as a dedicated "seeker," and enjoyed the fantasy that this put me into the center of everything exciting, critical, and significant. There were answers, and I was going to find them in this lifetime.

One day a friend handed me a book by Wei Wu Wei and asked me if I knew anything about it. He said he didn't understand it and wondered if I would read it to see what it was all about. In retrospect, I now see that nothing was accidental about this moment at all. I read the book that night from cover to cover. Two things stand out. First, I didn't have a clue what the book was about and second, I knew in my bones that I had been handed a gift. Unconsciously I knew exactly what the book was about—it made the hair on my arms stand straight up and my heart raced for no apparent reason. At the conscious level, I was permitted, thanks to denial, to grasp every ninth word if I was lucky. The book's style was very abstruse, even a bit pedantic and "Oxfordian," but the hidden message set off a firestorm of inquiry that persists to this day. That was over twenty-five years ago.

I have since read all of Wei Wu Wei's books, and I love them all like children. Each is an exquisite gem. I have also read everything everyone else said or thought about him. It is clear now that he had a profound impact on many seekers, including the great and wonderful Balsekar.

It is poetic justice that very little is known about Wei Wu Wei. This is certainly in keeping with his belief that there is no one to know anything about. What we do know is that he was born into a very affluent family in Ireland in the year 1895 and that he died at the age of ninety-one in 1986. Curiously, not unlike Siddartha, he left the fold to study, travel, and learn about life's great mysteries. His chief mentor was Sri Ramana Maharshi at Sri Ramanashram in Tiruvannamalai, India. At the age of sixty-three he published his first of eight books, which were released between 1958 and 1974. He also made contributions to a variety of periodicals, including *The Mountain Path,* as well as *The Middle Way,* and *Etre Libre,* a French periodical.

Psychology is all about working with people and their problems. Wei Wu Wei's interpretation of Buddhist philosophy shook the very foundation of all my beliefs, particularly those that apply to the dynamics of psychotherapy. Little did I know that I was going to engage in a long struggle between what we say is, and what might actually be. Little by little, materialism gave way to the truth that everything we refer to as reality isn't what we insist it is.

These new views forced me to alter the way I worked with people. As I began to see things differently, my practice shifted from the standard Western view of life to a much vaster view of existence as a dream in which everything we do is content in the dream. The shift was from real people in trouble to spirits in trouble trying to be real people. Denial saw to it this shift came very slowly, but the pull in this direction was as arresting as the ideas in Wei Wu Wei's books. There was no turning back. The whole process reminds me of waking up from a giant slumber, a trance that locks fiction into fact and fact into fiction. This metanoesis, as Wei Wu Wei refers to it, feels like a 180-degree shift in course, in which enlightenment happens to the dreamers in the dream and not to the dreamed figures who pretend to be real people.

–Dr. Gregory Tucker

Foreword

To any book on Metanoesis

A READER who firmly believes that he can reach any satisfactory understanding of himself and his relation to the universe which apparently surrounds him—*via* a self which he is conditioned to regard as an autonomous individual, is wasting his time in reading this book. He would need to be prepared to lay aside such a point of view and find that *as such* he has nothing but an apparent sentient existence which has no ultimate significance whatever, on account of the evident fact that he himself as a 'fact' and a 'self' does not exist at all.

Among the uncountable, because historically unknown, human beings who have come to understand what they are—that inconceivable immensity in comparison with their own insignificant 'appearance' (as phenomenon)—there are a few thousand on record, among whom a few hundred have left us some account of their awakened comprehension.

That immense and total understanding of what we sentient beings, each and all, human, animal and vegetable, are is the exclusive subject of this book; and it is based on what those who have come to understand what in fact they are, have told us about what they found and how they found it—which is also how we too may find it. That is done by understanding that what we appear to be is a fleeting shadow, a distorted and fragmentary reflection of what we all are when we no longer assume that we are that phenomenal appearance.

Why is it a joke? It is a joke because all the time we are nothing but the substance and have never for a moment been the fleeting and tormented shadow. It is comical also because whereas it is essentially simple and obvious, an immense series of structures, religious and philosophical, has been built in order to explain it. In these psychic constructions men and women quite often spend their adult lives elaborating devotional and sentimental, as well as intellectual, personalities which hinder rather than help this ultimate understanding, which in itself is neither of a devotional, a sentimental, nor an intellectual character, but is very precisely the transcending of each, and the rejection of all three.

Intellectually some degree of this understanding is neither uncommon nor difficult to acquire, relatively speaking at least, but only a minute fraction of those who have this intellectual understanding ever reach the totality of the understanding itself, which ultimately is what they are. The reason for this is that they cannot accept the absolute annihilation of what they have been conditioned to believe is their identity, and that such is only a phenomenon entirely devoid of substance of its own, as of any autonomy, an appearance dreamed as a dreamed-figure is dreamed, a shadow, a reflection, and no entity at all. They will often work hard, following techniques and methods, religious and laic, they will even devote their whole lives to it, or what remains of their lives. But all is to no purpose as long as they cling to the illusion that they themselves are entities working to some end. They succeed in comprehending the emptiness, the voidness of objective things, in fulfilling all the conditions laid down by the schools and the teachers, but as long as they 'themselves' are doing it, or even deliberately not-doing it, no matter what they may be *doing*, and no matter how apparently unselfish and 'holy' it may be, never can they achieve anything unless or until they have understood that it is because they 'themselves' are void, empty, and only apparently existent that their objects are such also.

All the anguish and despair they may experience is inevitable, but it is beside the point, because nothing whatever can be achieved by 'themselves' volitionally no matter what they may try to do or refrain from doing. Nearly always, save in the rare case, the so very rare case that need not be rare at all, they are working on objects, on phenomena, on other shadows in mind, instead of comprehending their own total inexistence as autonomous entities, which comprehension, by abruptly snapping the phenomenally interminable chain of conceptualisation, would reveal the noumenality whose immensity is all that they are.

Words themselves cannot bring this about, for words cannot define it, words as such are entirely a product of phenomenality and are limited by the boundaries of the phenomenal; words can only lead towards it, clear away superficial misunderstanding, and point in the right direction —which is away from everything that they themselves represent. But that initial clearance, that general understanding, that final indicating, are absolutely necessary, and are all that we in the West, who have no qualified Masters, can offer to one another in order that our eyes may be opened to the illusion represented by everything we are conditioned to imagine is 'ourselves'.

But words, however carefully chosen, rejected, screened, cannot, owing to their nature, fulfill their limited role as long as their reader takes them to 'himself', seeks to use them for 'himself', and sees the illusory character of everything in the Universe except that of the reader. Words are wasted if his total unsubstantiality, his own utter absence as what he is conditioned to think he is, as what he appears in his own eyes to be, as what other dreamed-figures consider him to be, is not the basis of every single insight that words may have enabled him to apprehend. That, believe me, is the *sine qua non:* without that analytical understanding, that profound and absolute conviction, that luminously clear and utterly evident apperception—words can never render up the subtle meaning that they may hold in suspense, though they may, nevertheless, help 'him' to reach this profound inseeing of his own total absence as any 'thing' but an appearance.

In a sense, too, he must do this *in spite of* words, for words can rarely point at noumenality without at the same time carrying a superficial and useless meaning when interpreted in a phenomenal context.

All that such a book as this could ever do is to provide psychological, and so conceptual, material, not widely accessible in modern idiom, whereby such a reader can come to a clear understanding of the teaching of the great awakened Masters, whose own words in a vanished context and idiom are often obscure as a result of the accidents of transmission and the lack of metaphysical understanding on the part of earnest and erudite translators.

This book is dedicated to every reader, that he may use it as best he may, which is by never forgetting that every reference to 'himself', every such noun or pronoun, *inevitable* if words are to convey meaning, does not in fact refer to a suppositional autonomous individual, unless specifically so stated, but to a *phenomenon* regarded as such, whose objective appearance can be named and described, but whose *noumenality* is all that he is.

P.S. Once more: any reader concerned with 'self-cultivation', with self-noughting, with 'improving himself', with working on or via what he believes to be some kind of entity which subjectively or objectively he is, will be wasting 'his' time in reading this book, as he will have wasted 'my' time in writing it. Unless, of course, in reading it he should come to apprehend that what is reading is not in fact an entity at all, but that reader, reading, and what is read are THIS, HERE, and NOW, which, neither entity nor non-entity, is the sought which is seeking, the seeker which is the sought.

ACKNOWLEDGEMENTS

Chapter 1, 'Metanoesis', Chapter 25, 'This—And All That', and Chapter 26, 'Without Tears' are reprinted by kind permission of the Editor of *The Mountain Path* (issues of July 1965, April 1965, and January 1965) Sri Ramanasramam, Tiruvannamali, S. India. Chapter 31, 'The Cube-Root of Zero', and Chapter 87, 'It May be Suggested' are reprinted hy kind permission of the Editor of *The Middle Way* (issues of May and November 1965), 58 Eccleston Square, London, S.W.1.

Contents

PART II

SELF AND OTHER

PART III

NON-OBJECTIVE RELATION

PART IV

TIME

PART V
ABSENCE

APPENDIX
TECHNICAL TERMS

INDEX

PART I

IDENTITY

It is only with total humility, and in absolute stillness of mind that we can know what indeed we are.

1. Metanoesis

I

EVERY QUESTION concerns you looking or not-looking, doing or not-doing, knowing or not-knowing;

Never the thing (object) looked-at, done, known; never *it's* being or not-being.

As long as there is you *doing*, it makes no difference whether there is doing or not-doing—for both are doing by you.

Paravritti, metanoesis, the '180 degree turn-over', is not a turning over by a 'doing or not-doing' you, a turning from positive to negative; it is not done by 'a you'. It is not done by any other 'entity' either. It is not done at all. It is the timeless, unceasing *prajñāic* functioning of our dhyānic non-being that becomes phenomenally present when there is neither doing nor non-doing, i.e. when there is 'fasting of the mind'.

It is not the object that is or is-not, but the cogniser of the thing that *either* is *or* is-not—that *neither* is *nor* is-not *as a cogniser*.

All looking, doing, cognising is the same process as looking for 'I' (the looker, doer, cogniser) as an object. Why? because a you (I) is looking, etc., and also because every object ultimately is I. The looking for 'I' as an object is the looking that is all looking for all objects; so is the not-looking for 'I' as an object the not-looking for any object whatever.

But it is the looker, rather than the object, that neither is nor is-not. Always, always, in every case and context.[1] Therefore it is only when you (I) cease looking that the total *absence* of the looking you (I) can be *present*—and that is the '180 degree turn'.

Who is looking? As long as a 'who' looks, objects can be seen only as objects, and a looking 'who' cannot be

---

[1] The object also, of course, which phenomenally either is or is-not, noumenally neither is nor is-not, but only because it is integral in its subject.

replaced by WHO? which neither is nor is-not, as long as he is looking.

Only in the absence of both looking and not-looking can a looking, which neither is nor is-not looking, be present. And such presence is you ('I').

Is not that the message of the Diamond and Heart Sutras?

II

Not clear enough? Let's look at it like this:

No object as such is *either* good *or* not good, which are attributes in the cognising of which by split mind there arises the supposition of a cogniser and of some thing cognised.

But there has never been a cogniser, and there has never been any thing cognised, object or attribute of object, which are split aspects of the *prajñāic* function*ing* which we are calling cognis*ing*.

Once one has been pulled, pushed or wheedled out of the notion that objects as such, and their attributes, are as we sensorially perceive and intellectually interpret them, and has apperceived that their objective existence, as well as ours, is entirely visionary, surely one can understand that all they are is their source?

What is a little more difficult to apprehend is that their source as such, subjectively, is all that even objectively they are.

Then, all that remains is to apperceive that what we are looking for is this which is looking.

2. *Identity of Dualism and Non-Dualism*

The Sage no longer differentiates between dualism and non-dualism *(advaita)*, for he does not cognise them as different.

Objective Godhead and Subjective Godhead are Identical

A self that prays, humbly,[1] to God, and a self that, being no longer personal, is God, are basically the same, so that praying humbly[1] to God, and being, impersonally, God, are not fundamentally different.

Being oneself, without self, is not different from 'oneself', without self, being 'other'.

That is why, to the Sage, there is no difference between self and other.

Thereafter the ultimate understanding of the Sage is: I am no longer an 'I', what that 'I' is-not is all there is, and this is Godhead.

Note: That, also, explains the three degrees of understanding in Buddhism: *(1)* when mountains and rivers are cognised as such: subject seeing object; *(2)* when mountains and rivers are no longer cognised as mountains and rivers: object seen as subject only; and *(3)* when mountains and rivers are once more cognised as mountains and rivers: subject and object seen as not separate. That is why 'the way' is often described as being discrimination between object and subject: so that, temporarily, objects may no longer be cognised as objects.

[1] 'Humbly' here is not used as the counterpart of 'proudly', for such 'humility' is just negative 'pride'. Humility, metaphysically, implies the absence of any entity to be either 'proud' or 'humble'.

3. *What is Mind?*

I

THE SENSORIALLY-PERCEIVED universe is *thereby* the objective aspect of mind. Mind has no other objective aspect at all. That is to say that it has no objective existence as 'mind'.

Whereas, objectively, mind is not otherwise than as the sensorially-perceived universe, subjectively it cannot *be* anything else either. Since what itself is subjectively cannot be any kind of 'thing', it cannot *be* other than what it is in objectivisation.

Since there can be no kind of 'thing' for it to be, mind must necessarily be whatever we are that so-perceive the manifested universe.

Therefore, since both objectively and subjectively the manifested universe is 'mind' and vice-versa, the manifested universe is whatever we are both objectively and subjectively. Nowhere herein is there any place for duality: objectivity dissolves in subjectivity, and subjectivity has no cognisable existence other than as objectivity.

This amounts to inseeing that Apperceiving is whatever we are, and that whatever we are is Apperceiving. This, no doubt, may be regarded as the functional aspect of inbeing, or *prajñā* as the functional aspect of *dhyāna*.

That, surely, is why Suchness is So?

II

In Nineteen Plain Words

EVERYTHING COGNISED is just what is called 'mind',
And what is called 'mind' is just the cognising of everything.

Who done it? No Jack-in-the-box anywhere!
So what is there left to write about?

Note: (1) Two very simple little statements, even rather obvious? But don't let us be deceived by their simplicity. Perhaps if one were to look into them deeply enough the dawn itself might break?

Note: (2) Huang Po on this subject, *cassant* as usual:

'Therefore it is said 'Perceiving a phenomenon IS perceiving Universal Nature, since phenomena and Mind are one and the same.' (p. 118)

'Those who in their single-minded attempt to reach Buddhahood, detest the sentient world, thereby blaspheme all the Buddhas of the Universe.' (p. 130)

'My advice to you is to rid yourselves of all your previous ideas about *ctudying* Mind or *perceiving* it.' (p. 130)

'On no account make a distinction between the Absolute and the sentient world.' (p. 130)

4. *What is Mind?*

III

'Champagne Charlie'

THIS GLASS of champagne, I see its colour, I hear its sparkle, I inhale its bouquet, I taste its savour, I feel its coolness and formlessness, and I know its quality. In fact I completely cognise it.

What have I cognised? Champagne. But what is that? A concept, champagne-concept. What could that be apart from the cognising of it? Surely it is no thing whatever *apart from the cognising of it?* What else could there be for it to be? If it were something else, how could I know that it was something else, or what that was? Only by cognising. Have I any other way of knowing anything?

Then what cognised it? An indefinable concept called 'mind' cognised it. What is this indefinable concept? Being a concept, it too is cognising—'cognising' cognising 'cognising'?

It is THIS which cognises? What else could it be? And if it were something else, how could I ever know that it is something else, or what that is? What else could there be to know that or anything whatever?

So 'mind' is what cognises, and what is cognised is 'mind'. And they are 'this'—this which cognises and that which is cognised.

Where do I come in? I must be 'this and that', subject and object! Evidently, inevitably I must be *this* 'mind' which appears to be the cogniser, and *that* champagne which appears to be the cognised, the cogniser and the cognised, both and neither, all and no thing.

'I' am Champagne Charlie!

Note: What are you saying? It is wine, made from grapes, dextrose and levulose transformed by ferments into alcohol, acid, carbonic acid gas, etc., etc.? Is it indeed? And how do you know that? Memory? And what is all that? Concepts. Results of cognition, what is termed 'knowledge'. 'Cognising' cognising—'cognising'.

5. *Every Psyche Has Her Soma*

YES, INDEED, and every Soma has his Psyche. There has never been the one without the other, or the other without the one. A pretty pair of phenomenal counterparts, a very pretty couple of concepts, still imperfectly cognised, particularly the young lady. Otherwise much like all the other interdependent complementaries.

But there is one thing odd about them, quite exceptional: they are cognised as one and called a 'self', whereas, like all the others, they are only identical in their mutual negation.

That is what is wrong.

6. Closing-in. I

For Professor Walter Liebenthal

PRAJÑĀ

PRAJÑĀ IS Light, seeking out darkness and never finding it, for wherever Light is, darkness vanishes, since darkness is absence of the presence of Light.

Prajñā is Knowing, seeking ignorance and never finding it, for wherever Knowing is, ignorance vanishes, since ignorance is absence of the presence of Knowing.

Prajñā is Functioning, seeking repose and never finding it, for wherever Functioning is, repose vanishes, since repose is absence of the presence of Functioning.

Prajñā is Subject, seeking object, all seeking for all that is sought, and never finding it, for wherever Seeking Subject is, the object sought vanishes, since the object sought is absence of the presence of Subject Seeking.

7. *Closing-in. II*

Finding the Seeker

WHEN LIGHT seeks out Darkness,
The only finding is understanding that what has been
    'found'
Was the absence of that which was seeking.

All that a Seeker can find is his own absence,
For this which is seeking is all there could have been
    to be found.

Asking 'Who am I?', therefore, is the Light
Searching for the Darkness of a 'me',
And finding that there is no 'Who?',
But only the absence of the presence of this-which-
    is-asking.

Note: Why does Light seek out Darkness? Because there is nothing else
in the Cosmos which it has not found.

II

IN REPOSE, it is pure potentiality;
Functioning, it must seek itself as other,
In order to find that the absence of other
Is the absence which itself is.

For there is no self that is not other,
And no other that is not self;
Nor anywhere in the Cosmos
Can there be anything that is other than self.

Having found no self that is not other,
The seeker must find that there is no other that is not
    self,
So that in the absence of both other and self
There may be known the perfect peace
Of the presence of absolute absence.

8. *Closing-in. III*

Identity

Could there be other-than-self
That has not, does not need or know, a self?
Could there be self
That has not, needs not or does not know, other-
than-self?

Seeking for himself,
What could self find but other,
Seeking for other,
What could self find but himself?

For other is the absence of self,
And self is the absence of other.

9. When Mind Fasts . . .

Discoursively Presented

'SELF' and 'OTHER' are two empty concepts, each totally lacking in verisimilitude, making sense only in their interdependence as appearances in mind.

There is no self, there is no other-than-self. No thing of the kind exists at all except as phenomenon.

All they are is what they are when they are not anything. Objectively figments, they represent mind cognising them within itself, and the cognising of them is itself their phenomenal being.

To differentiate between them is absurd; to be identified with one and to regard the other as independent is ridiculous; to claim one and to reject the other is the purblind nonsense of identification—for all each is, is whatever I am, and whatever I am is all that anything is.

'That' is no other than 'this', and 'this' is no other than either, for each is the cognising of both, and such is what I am.

Self and other are images extended in conceptual space and in conceptual time (duration), rendered apperceptible as phenomena thereby, and their only being lies in their interdependent apprehending.

To a sage, differentiation into self and other-than-self is just the 'let's pretend' of children playing at being Judy and Punch.

Dialectically

10. *Apperceiving the Identity of all Opposites*

JUST AS by the superimposition of positive and negative in photographic films the opposing elements of light and shade complement one another, thereby producing mutual annihilation, so is it with all interdependent counterparts, negative and positive concepts, sometimes called opposites or complementaries.

It matters not whether we are making concepts about *samsāra* and *nirvāna*, object and subject, phenomenon and noumenon, other and self, presence and absence, for all represent aspects of the division of mind in the process of conceptualisation which is termed dualism. The absence of this process—non-dualism, *advaita*,—which implies pre-conceptualisation, mind upstream of all conceptualising—is a return to wholeness of mind, which is called 'the truth of Ch'an'. That implies disidentification with a phenomenal object, a psyche-soma, which is picturesquely referred to as 'enlightenment', or liberation from the supposed bondage which appears to result from that identification.

Such identification entails a conceptual splitting of whole *prajñāic* apperceiving into a pseudo-subject cognising a pseudo-object, and that process results in the apparent condition of bondage. Therein the subjective element is always the negative, and the objective always the positive; *nirvāna*, noumenon, self, absence, being negative, and *samsāra*, phenomenon, other, presence, the positive; and in every case their assimilation results in a mutual negation which abolishes each as either, and leaves a situation which is void of any conceptual element except voidness itself.

It is not different if we seek to conceptualise the self-contradictory opposites such as non-being and being, non-manifestation and manifestation, non-acting and acting, and so on *ad infinitum:* the former are negative, their counterparts positive, and their assimilation results in the mutual cancellation of each. It should be noted, however, that in no case are two thoughts united, for no such operation is psychologically possible; mutually contradictory concepts just negate and so abolish one another in a third concept of voidness, so that wholeness results only from the cancellation of a conceptual division, and such wholeness is conceptually a void. There is clearly no 'middle path' here, and that absurd and pedantic translation is a misleading obnubilation of the process which has just been described.

However, we are still left with a concept holding us 'bound'—that of 'voidness'. Let us take two examples.

When presence and absence as such are assimilated, there is no longer either presence or absence, for each counteracts the nature of the other and annihilates it.

The essential negation, however, is the absence of that resultant absence. This further negation, or double absence, is the absence of (that sort of absence which is) the absence of presence. And that alone is what is implied by 'Suchness'.[1]

So many great Masters have assured us that the complete apprehension of this initial identity of conceptual opposites, even of any one such pair, is itself liberation, saying that to 'see' one is to 'see' all, that we should not fail to recognise the importance of this apperception. Its perfect apprehension, we are told, should result in im-mediate disidentification with the pseudo (phenomenal) subject of pseudo (phenomenal) objects, both of which are just concepts devoid of 'ens', whose mutual abolition reveals the *prajñāic* functioning which is all suchness.

Note: Since authority is reassuring to some people, the above will be found to be a discursive application of the principle of the double negative of Shen Hui, and of what has been so clearly and repeatedly told us by the most familiar and best-translated Masters, such as Huang Po and Hui Hai, and should be a statement in current language of the burden of the Diamond and Heart Sutras of the *Prajñāpāramitā*.

[1] It might seem to be simpler just to say that the essential negation is that of whatever is conceptualising these absences, but the Masters sometimes considered it helpful to carry on logical or dialectic negation to its limit.

11. *Analytical. I*

DISCOURSIVE, DIALECTIC, or discriminative analysis of the so-called 'opposites' and 'complementaries' can treat all of them objectively, that is as nouns, and in every case their mutual reintegration psychologically will leave the resultant concept of 'voidness'. All can be grouped and examined under the single aspect of Negative-Positive.

The abolition of the resultant concept of 'voidness', however, can only be effected by its negation when the nominal dualities are grouped under the pronominal or personal I and personal You, for such resultant voidness is, precisely, personal voidness, and its negation must necessarily be the negation of the subject as well as of the object.

All the pairs of so-called 'opposites' and 'complementaries' can be grouped under the pair I and You, and so regarded noumenally instead of phenomenally, that is pre-conceptually and non-objectively. The expression in dualistic language of such im-mediate apperceiving necessarily remains superficially dualistic, but basically it is non-dialectical, non-discriminative, and non-discoursive. On this account it is not dialectically logical, and could never be such, and it can only be apprehended by im-mediate apperceiving.

Noumenal apperceiving indicates apperceiving pre-conceptually, at the undivided source of phenomenality. It requires no rationalisation, no reification, but just apperceiving unscrambled by dialectical interference. Therefore this apprehending, directly apperceived, can only indirectly be recorded, and never discoursively.

Under the personal pronoun 'I' are grouped all the negative elements, to which this pronoun can be applied, and under the personal pronoun 'YOU' all the positive elements, as follows:

'A'	'B'
I	*YOU*
Self	Other
Subject	Object
Noumenon	Phenomena
Nirvāna	*Samsāra*
Negative	Positive
Absence	Presence
Voidness	Plenum
Non-being	Being
Non-manifestation	Manifestation
Non-action	Action
*Y*IN	*Y*ANG
Etc. etc.	Etc. etc.

There are three degrees of cognising:

(1) Perceiving phenomenally

(2) Perceiving noumenally

(3) Apperceiving non-dually, upstream of conceptualisation.

Phenomenal cognising consists of phenomenal subject perceiving phenomenal objects,

Noumenal cognising consists of phenomenality cognised subjectively,

Non-dual cognising apprehends phenomenality and noumenality as not separate, which implies the dissolution of all opposites and complementaries, and is pre-conceptual.

12. Analytical. II

IN THE photographic analogy three-dimensional objects are recorded on a two-dimensional plane-surface, light and shade being reversed, and the third dimension being represented by occular perspective. This negative record is then mechanically reversed, thereby producing a two-dimensional positive which represents in perspective the three-dimensional objects recorded.

In the case of sensorial perception/conception the analogy holds good. Four-dimensional apperceptions are translated into three-dimensional concepts, the fourth direction of measurement being represented by the passage of time (duration), also via a negative which is then visualised as a positive, and in both cases a positive image is restored.

For instance an aspect of Suchness (as we have to refer to it, being unable to know anything four-dimensional as such) is translated as a negative concept, and its positive counterpart immediately appears. When this process is reversed the positive is applied to its negative, each annihilates the other, and the resultant phenomenally is the inevitable four-dimensional voidness of 'neither . . . nor . . .' that cannot be visualised but which noumenally carries a positive implication which nevertheless cannot be a three-dimensional concept.

The most familiar examples of the latter process are the Ch'an series of *wu hsin, wu nien, wu wei,* etc., mind, thought, action, etc. returned to their negatives no-mind, no-thought, no-action, which mutually negated imply, that is point directly to, the pure four-dimensional non-objectivity that cannot otherwise be described, or be conceived or named without thereby turning it back into a positive concept. This, therefore, can only be referred to, described or indicated in some such terms as 'mind that is no-mind', 'absolute thought', 'action of non-action or non-volitional action'—all perfectly illogical and inacceptable indications within the limits of our dimensionally-restricted powers of conceptualisation.

Note: It may be desirable to remember that each direction of measurement is at right-angles to *all others*, and that each greater dimension includes all lesser.[1] Therefore a further and unknown direction, which cannot be visualised from the known, here a fourth from the third, can only be *suggested* by the 'within' of Jesus, and all we can objectively know of it is that it includes the three that we are able to use.

Mathematics can play symbolically with dimensions *ad libitum*, but what may thereby be represented is difficult to imagine. In the present example the fourth and all-inclusive is the noumenal where tri-dimensional phenomenality is concerned—as, no doubt, our third would be the noumenal to duo-dimensional beings.

It is evident that the term 'phenomenal' covers all our psycho-physical appearance in three directions of measurement, and that 'noumenality' refers to whatever we may be in a further direction in which the phenomenal is entirely included. This is, therefore, an all-inclusive continuum.

All basic measuring is from here to there; all measurements have a point from which they are made. Ultimately that point is inevitably I, and so whatever I may be.

Therefore I am the point of departure of all dimensions. And as each is at right-angles to all others I must be their mutual centre wherever and whenever that may be.

Finally, since each greater surface or volume embraces all lesser areas I must be the centre of the continuum which all seek to measure.

[1] Time can be seen to include the three spatial dimensions.

13. Analytical. III

The All-Embracing Measure

'DIMENSIONS' ARE merely our conceptual extension in 'Space', which appears in three divergent directions of measurement as length, breadth, and height, a fourth, spatially incognisable but called 'voidness', being phenomenally represented by duration.

It is this latter which represents our apparent being, for we appear to exist because we appear to last. Our continuation in time, long or short, our growth and development therein, our process of being born, maturing, ageing and dying *seems* to take place, or be extended as we say, in 'time', so that what we are is seen to be that lasting, becoming, in the framework of 'space'.

Our appearance must be dependent on the concepts of 'space' and 'time', for without them we could not appear to be, and without us they are not at all. They are our apparent extension, three directions of measurement conceived as spatial dimensions, the fourth as temporal.

As has been demonstrated herein, there is no past, no future, and the 'present', i.e. existence as such, is no moment, but is this temporal dimension which includes all the others, and so represents what we can be said to be.

Being is Becoming

'Absolute voidness devoid of differentiation', as envisaged by Nāgārjuna, is represented by this further all-embracing continuum.

As is also what is called 'Buddha-mind', and ours.

It is termed 'mind' or 'heart' *(hsin),*

It is Suchness too, and it is *Nirvāna*, and Noumenon.

We can only speak of it correctly in the first-person-singular, for it is no 'thing', is objectively nil, but we know it as 'Eternity', as duration, as becoming.

So we are what 'time' is, and what 'time' is we are,
And 'time' is the all-embracing measure of space.

14. Light on the Subject

LIGHT SHINES: it does not seek to shine; it does not know that it is shining; it just appears to shine on encountering objective resistance, and shining is all that it appears to be.

Shining, therefore, is the apparent nature, the apparent being of the suchness of Light. And wherever it is shining it never finds darkness—but always itself.

Light in itself is insentient and incognisable, invisible, inaudible, intangible; light is ubiquitous in space although the sky itself appears dark. Sensorially, in manifestation, imperceptible, as light it may be said to have no conceptual existence apart from its shining, but is cognisable only by objective reflection from sensorially perceived particles in our conceptually assumed atmosphere.

All this, however, merely happens to *us*, or appears to happen or not to happen, to *us*. We think, and say, that it 'exists' merely because it is among the experiences that are sensorially perceptible to sentient beings, among reactions recorded by one or more of our five rudimentary senses and interpreted by the sixth. It appears to happen to us: that is all we can know about it; the assumption that it has any other existence whatever, to suggest that it exists in any manner or degree independently of our cognising of it, is entirely gratuitous. Therefore to think or to speak of it as being this, that, the other, anything whatever or nothing, is merely absurd. All we can ever know of it is what we ourselves think about it; it exists, therefore, as an appearance in our psyche, and it has no known or knowable existence of its own.

'Light' is *our* light: and there is no reason whatever to suppose that there is any other kind of light. And so, being our light, it is an aspect of whatever-we-are; being nothing whatever but whatever-we-are, we must be what it is, and since whatever-we-are must always be reduced to the vocable 'I', no matter who says it, Light must be I, and I must be Light. Therefore whatever Light may be, I arise and shine. But I only manifest when I encounter the apparent resistance of objectivity, whereby I shine, for when all apparent objects are removed, objects and I remain in the potentiality of *Dhyāna*, the static aspect of *Prajñā*, which is the not-shining of Light and the apparent darkness of space.

In whatever direction light may be oriented, on whatever resistance it may manifest and shine, it never finds darkness, but always its own light; in whatever direction I may be oriented—all sentience being 'I'—never can I find other than I, for whether or not I manifest and shine, I never encounter darkness, but only absence of my light as 'I'. My presence and my absence, therefore, have none but an apparent difference due to the apparent existence of objects, for there is nothing but what I am as Suchness.

Every shining action which is the apparent aspect of the functioning of Light, finds only itself—for nothing can be perceived that is not illumined by *Prajñā* which I am. Darkness is a concept which entails absence of light, which is the voidness of annihilation. Only in the eternal and ubiquitous shining of timeless and spaceless *Prajñā* can there be sentience, and sentience can be said to be a distributed radiance of *prajñāic* shining, finding expression dualistically via supposedly independent entities, whose apparent independent existence is a conceptual effect of such divided reflection.

The luminosity of *prajñāic* functioning, which to every sentient being is 'I', renders every action universal—since only the luminous functioning of *prajñāic* 'I' can produce the appearance of action. The supposed individuals concerned may be regarded as phenomenal reflections in whom the *prajñāic* shining is all that they are and all that the vocable 'I' can be assumed to imply.

Therefore by 'the seeing' of you, you can see me; in 'the hearing' of the stream, you can hear the stream; in 'the cognising' of the sensorial universe, every sentient being can cognise the universe; and in 'the apprehending' of 'the truth of Ch'an', every sentient being can apprehend it—and so can be 'free'.

It is what I am that is seeing,
And I have ten-thousand eyes.

Non-dialectically

15. Prajnā and the Sage

ALL THE sage is—is *prajnā;*
All the sage was, before he became a sage, *was prajnā,*
Split into subject and object.

However, there is no *prajnā,*
And there is no sage.
There is not either the one or the other,
Either both, or neither:
Just a luminous absence.

But light is a concept of divided mind,
And absence is absence of presence.
Whatever they are not, whatever they are,
Cannot be known by whatever they are
Or by whatever they are not,
For there is no knower to know anything,
Nor any thing to be known.

16. How?

I CANNOT KNOW what I am,
For that would need a knower to know it.
I can only be; unconscious of being at all?

But then there would still be an I, an I that *is*,
And that is unconscious of something that *is*
And is called *being*.

How could there be any thing at all,
Either being or I?

Where could there be for any thing to be
Extended in space?
When could there be for any thing to be
Extended in time?

Who?

I cannot *say* it,
I cannot *know* it,
I cannot *be* it.

Because I *am* it,
And all it is I am.

17. Presence and Absence

PHENOMENALLY I am always present,
Because phenomena are what objectively I am.
Phenomenally I *appear* to be absent,
Because my presence as phenomena
Conceals my phenomenal absence as noumenon.

Noumenally I am neither present nor absent,
Because presence and absence are phenomenal concepts
Inapplicable to noumenality, which is the absence
Of the absence of phenomenal presence,
Which is no-absence.

Noumenally, therefore, I am unmanifesting potentiality,
Objectively absent because unobjectifiable,
Subjectively absent because not objectifying,
Doubly absent, because absent both as subject and as object.

When I act, I act as *Prajñā*,
And I manifest as the phenomenal universe.
Then I am present.

18. Non-Conceptuality

WHAT-WE-ARE cannot be comprehended because there cannot be any comprehender apart from what-we-are to comprehend what-we-are. If a comprehender could comprehend itself there would be a subject comprehender and its object comprehended, and the comprehending subject would again become an object, the object of a comprehender. A perpetual regression is then reached, as always.

Must not what-we-are, then, *be* that perpetual regression, the perpetual regression of subject becoming the object of a subject *ad infinitum*? Dialectically, dualistically, phenomenally, it must surely be so, for phenomenon is the appearance of noumenon which thereby itself becomes a conceptual appearance, or phenomenon, of noumenon, *ad infinitum*. Zenith has a Nadir which must have a Zenith, and so with all opposites and all complementaries for ever and ever.

That is surely why Shen Hui proclaimed the double negative, the absence of the absence of presence-and-absence, the absence of that (kind of) absence which is neither presence nor absence.

That is only a dialectical wheeze to get out of duality by means of duality? Perhaps it is. But out we must be got, for duality is the mechanism of bondage. Surely, however, it is not the concept that matters, but the fact that there always remains the conceiver of the concept, whatever it may be? And he it is who is bound. He, also, it is who *is not*, never has been and never could be, to be bound or anything else.

But he cannot even say 'I am not' for in saying it he demonstrates that he is. Nor can he get out of himself by saying that he is everything, for every*thing* is as much a thing as no*thing*, and he is still a conceiver conceiving himself as one or the other or both or neither. Yet again he cannot be rid of himself by claiming transcendence, for then something transcends something else, and that remains as the transcender.

Can he disappear by means of immanence? Something remains immanent, some thing however tenuous and vague that dwells within something more solid, an absence within a presence. Even the most impersonal immanence as such is an objective concept, and that objective concept has a subject, which thereby becomes an object—and so on *ad infinitum*.

Does this demonstrate that it is dialectically, conceptually impossible to comprehend what-we-are? Having apperceived that the absence of the absence of nothing is the clearest indication of what non-conceptually we are, we can only abandon the search, and that, if it be an abandonment also of the seeker, is *finding*. It is finding that the seeker is the sought, the sought is the seeker, and that neither is, was, ever could be, or is not, was not, or ever could not be, for each is the conceptual half of THIS which cannot be conceived, since THIS can never conceive itself without splitting into subject and object.

This conceptual not-ness is commonly regarded as some kind of catastrophe! But whyever should that be so? Surely it is no calamity not to be a concept? Is it not ridiculous, rather, to imagine that what-we-are could ever be a fugitive imponderability?

Is it not the conceivable that is negligible, dream-stuff, whereas the voidness, conceptually, which we are is necessarily plenitude in non-conceptuality? That is not conceptual darkness, but in non-conceptuality is light, light which darkness can never know, since darkness is nothing but absence of light.

What we are phenomenally, what we appear to be, is conceptual, therefore what we are non-conceptually is non-conceptuality as such, and if conceptually that is forever unknowable within the apparent confines of space and time, non-conceptually it is the not-knowing of knowing, non-finite and intemporal, neither anything nor nothing.

It cannot *be* cognised, precisely because what-we-are is we who are cognising, and 'cognising' cannot cognise 'cognising'.

Note: Phenomenally, split, we can be said to be what is conceptualising, and the concepts conceived; noumenally, un-split, we are up-stream of conceptualisation, and can neither conceive nor be conceived.

Therefore the difference, dualistically expressed, is that as phenomena what we are is conceptuality, and noumenally, non-conceptuality.

It is important to remember that 'we' do not conceptualise, for there is no 'we' as such, but that *what we are* is what is cognised as 'conceptualising'.

It seems to you odd that what we are should be described as 'conceptualisation'? Not odd, just factual. What else *could* we be?

19. *Boomerang*

I AM confused. . . .
About what?

The doctrine.
Inevitably: there isn't any.

I mean about how things work. . . .
They don't.

Well, then, about how and what we are?
There can be no how or what: we aren't.

Then about I am and I am not. . . .
I neither am nor am not.

YOU neither are nor are not?
I; you simply are not.

All right, then, this which I neither am nor am not, and that
which you simply are not.
What is there left to be confused about?

So that is it?
There is no 'it'.

Then what is the use of words?
They are perfect.

As what?
A boomerang.

20. *Bewildering Bits and Painful Pieces. I*

LIGHT DOES not *find* the Darkness of a 'me' because the Darkness of a 'me' was never anything but the absence of Light.

         ✧   ✧   ✧

We are miserable unless the sun is shining, but if the sun were shining within we should not even notice whether the feeble phenomenal sun was shining or not.

         ✧   ✧   ✧

It needs supreme humility in order to understand, and absolute silence of the mind. It might even be said that absolute humility IS understanding. Why? What does 'humility' signify except absence of consciousness of self?

         ✧   ✧   ✧

'You have no need to seek deliverance, since you are not bound'.
Hui Hai speaking.

         ✧   ✧   ✧

Turn the light on to yourself—and, believe me, you'll find nothing there.

         ✧   ✧   ✧

Fear, desire, affectivity are manifestations of the pseudo-entity which constitutes pseudo-bondage.
It is the entity, rather than the manifestations, thereof, which has to be eliminated.

         ✧   ✧   ✧

'I' is a part, but I am the whole.

         ✧   ✧   ✧

However fast you run after it, you will never catch it; however fast you run away from it, you will never lose it.

There can be no 'I' because there is no other-than-I.

❖   ❖   ❖

I cannot become what I am.
An eye sees, but does not look.
I look.

❖   ❖   ❖

The Individual As He Is

There is no other self to know the self of an individual self than the self which he is.

(Since the 'individual' is inseparable from what-he-is, like flame and fire, there is no self to know the individual except the self which is inseparable from what-he-is.)

(Paraphrase of Maharshi from 'Self Enquiry')

❖   ❖   ❖

The quality called 'humility' refers to the lack of anyone to possess it.

❖   ❖   ❖

'*You* cannot see it because *you* are transparent.' (stop reading until you see what this means).

❖   ❖   ❖

I am the awareness of being aware that I am universal awareness, the first dim, the second brilliant, the last a blinding radiance.

❖   ❖   ❖

Beware of *beatified individuality.*

PART II

SELF AND OTHER

Every sentient being, speaking as I, may say to his phenomenal self, 'Be still! and know that I am God!'

21. *The Big Joke*

I

As LONG as there is a 'you' doing or not-doing anything, thinking or not-thinking, 'meditating' or 'not-meditating', *you* are no nearer home than the day *you* were 'born'.

However many years *you* may have been at it, and whatever *you* have understood or have not-understood, *you* have not yet started if there is a 'you' that is still in the saddle.

As long as *you* do anything as from a 'you', *you* are in 'bondage'.

Here the word *you* stands for any object that appears to act or not to act, that is any phenomenon as such. 'You' stands for any such object which believes that it acts volitionally as an autonomous entity, and is thereby bound by identification with a phenomenon.

Let us say it again: as long as there is a pseudo-entity apparently doing or not-doing anything, thinking or not-thinking, meditating or not-meditating, that phenomenon is no nearer home than the day it was apparently born.

However many years a phenomenon may have been at it, and whatever it has understood or not-understood, it has not yet started if there is a pseudo-entity that is still in the saddle.

As long as a phenomenon does anything *as from* a pseudo-entity, it is in 'bondage'.

The difference is between what you are and what you think you are but are not, 'bondage' being identification of the former with the latter.

Again: the difference is between This which every phenomenon is and That which no phenomenon is, 'bondage' being identification of the former with the latter.

That, in very simple language, is the pseudo-mystery, the so-called insoluble problem, the joke that made Lazarus Laugh.

II

TREATING THIS matter in the first person singular, it becomes a question of what we mean when we say 'I'.

If in saying 'I' we speak as from a psycho-somatic phenomenon that believes itself to be an independent entity acting or not-acting autonomously as a result of its own volition, then no matter what we may know or ignore, what we may have practised or not-practised, we are well and truly in bondage.

If in saying 'I'—although we may speak as from a phenomenon that appears to act or not to act (as observed by other phenomena and by 'itself')—we do not regard that phenomenon as possessing of its own right and nature any autonomy or volition, and so is properly to be regarded not as 'I' but as 'it', then since such phenomenon is not 'in the saddle' I am not identified with it, and I am not in bondage.

In this latter case the word 'I' is subjective only, as the word 'Je' in French, and for the accusative (or objective) case the word 'me' is necessary, as is 'moi' in French, even after the verb 'to be', for 'I' have no objective quality whatever, and all that could be called 'me' can never in any circumstances have any subjective quality, so that what I am as 'I' is purely noumenal and what I appear to be as 'me' is exclusively phenomenal. So that in saying 'I', if we speak or act as from what we are—from impersonal noumenality, with the spontaneity that is called 'Tao', there is no longer any question of bondage, for there is *no longer any supposed entity to be bound*.

III

THERE IS a further stage of fulfilment, in which complete reintegration takes place. Therein 'I' and 'it', 'I' and 'you', subject and object, lose all elements of difference. Of this stage only the fully integrated can be qualified to speak with authority, for herein no differentiation any longer is possible.

I am you, you are I, subject is object, and object subject, each is either and either is both, for phenomena are noumenon and noumenon is phenomena.

This is the end of the big joke, the final peal of laughter, for it, too, is so simple and obvious that only the blindfold should fail to see it, or could see it in any other manner.

Said as we say it, however that may be, it can never be true; said as the integrated say it, however that may be—even in the self-same words—it cannot be false: for what is neither false nor true cannot be false as it cannot be true. It is what it is—and whatever it be called, that it can never be.

22. *Prajnā*

WHEN CONTACT is made, by means of a switch, the electric current flows, the wire is instantly 'alive', the resistance becomes white-hot, and there is light.

When the contact is broken, the current no longer flows, the resistance cools, there is darkness, and the line is 'dead'.

The electric current is what is implied by *'prajnā'* where sentient beings are concerned: it is the act of action, the living of life.

Nobody knows what electricity is, nobody knows what *prajnā* is: both terms are just names given to concepts that seek to describe in dualistic language a basic 'energy' that enables appearance to appear and being to be.

When contact is made we know it as 'light' and as 'life'; when contact is broken we know it as 'darkness' and as 'death'. But the source of 'energy' remains intact and intangible.

Are we the hot resistance and the light, the cold resistance and the darkness—or the vital current itself?

23. *The Loud Laugh*

Is IT not all a great joke—which has been made a mystification by the devotionally-minded, no doubt because the suffering consequent on identification with a pseudo-entity (which so deeply impressed The Buddha), invites compassion (affectivity)?

But it is the huge joke that we should see, and loud laughter that should greet the seeing, for it is the simplicity and the obviousness of it, in contrast with the monumental superstructure of superfluous mystification that has been built round it, that calls forth the laughter.

The Ch'an Masters saw this, and said it? Saw it they certainly did, but they rarely did more than imply it. They were monks in monasteries and had their own particular conditioning. But whenever the sudden seeing of it was greeted with laughter by the see-er—the Master joined in the jest.

In a sense all Ch'an practice tends towards this irreverent revelation, for devotion is limitation, and so a binding, like any other. A superficial scaffolding of religiosity was maintained by these outwardly pious Buddhists, but the essential irreverence of their teaching, of their *wen-ta* (Jap. *mondo*), was the method by which they taught.

This is still the case to-day as regards the devotional background, but the reverential element has re-established itself at the expense of the straight-seeing, and to just that degree Ch'an has lost its efficacy and its appeal.

Philosophy can only reach it when the limit of rationality (dialectics) is reached, and the philosopher allows himself to pass over into pure metaphysics.

24. *Completion*

As LONG as there is a 'self' there are 'others'; as long as there are 'others' there is a 'self'.

As soon as there is no longer a 'self' there are no longer any 'others'; and as soon as there are no longer any 'others' there is no longer a 'self'.

But 'others' cannot be abolished by a 'self' *(or vice versa)*, nor can a 'self' be abolished by a 'self', because the 'self' to be abolished is then an 'other' to the 'self' that would abolish it.

'Self' and 'others' cannot be abolished—for abolition requires an abolisher. But 'self and others' being inter-dependent phenomenal counterparts, their complement produces mutual negation, the absence of which represents This-which-we-are.

Note: Just as negative and positive, subject and object, light and shade, so self and other mutually complement one another, thereby producing non-objectivity in which neither is either, and the non-objectivity that can be said to remain represents This-which-we-are.

25. 'This'—and All That

IN DUALISTIC language 'I' just stands for the Latin 'Ego' which is a concept without any factual existence, i.e. a complex which must be resolved because its psychological presence constitutes bondage. But, used as a metaphysical term, it implies This-which-we-are as opposed to That-which-we-think-we-are but are not.

That which is sensorially perceptible is *demonstrably* only an image in mind and, as such, can have no nature of its own. But the sentience of every sentient being must have a centre via which its functioning is directed, this 'centre' of each sentient object being as purely phenomenal as the sentient appearance. Such centre is devoid of volition, as of autonomy of any kind; it is not, therefore, an 'ego', and it cannot think self-consciously as 'I'.

Identification of This-which-we-are with each phenomenal object, in the process of objectifying this 'functional' centre, translates it as an individual 'ego-self', and so produces a suppositional 'entity'.

A phenomenon is a manifestation, and therefore an aspect, of noumenon. Spontaneous phenomenal action is noumenal, and so-living is noumenal living. Such, then, is non-identified living. It is identification with a spurious (imagined) autonomous *entity* that is supposed to be born, to suffer, and to die, that incurs the process of Causality called *karma*, and causes the notion of being in bondage to arise.

Phenomena as such, having no entity to be bound, cannot be bound, but neither have they an entity to be free. Always it is the 'entity' that is spurious, the phenomenon being what its name states—an appearance in mind, neither bound nor free.

The apparent problem, therefore, only concerns identification: it is identification that produces the notion of bondage. Identification with a phenomenal object results in the suppositional concept of an autonomous entity, and that concept is taken to be a factual 'self', whereas nothing of the kind exists, has ever existed, or ever could exist as a thing-in-itself, or as other than a concept in what is called 'mind'.

But identification with a phenomenal object as such is not *ipso facto* bondage, for such phenomenon has no 'ens' and need not have any—as may be observed in the case of a disidentified Sage who appears to live as any other man 'lives', at any rate to a casual observer.

It is only the superimposition of the elaborated concept of an autonomous self that is responsible for the notion of 'karma' and 'bondage', which are the effects of an apparent 'volition'.

II

LET US develop this understanding in greater detail. Noumenality has no need to identify itself with phenomenality, any more than an egg need be identified with an egg, nor need This-which-we-are identify itself with That-which-we-are, since their differentiation is one of objective appreciation only. But an identification of noumenality, not with phenomenality but with discriminated, or separated phenomena, entails the splitting into subject and object of phenomenality and the attribution of subjectivity to what is purely objective. That pseudo-subjectivity is attributed to the 'functional' centre of each separate phenomenal object, and this produces the idea of an autonomous individual with an ego-self.

Otherwise expressed, phenomenality being integral in noumenality, it must be the discrimination of phenomenality into separate phenomena possessed of both subjective and objective character that produces identification. Such identification, then, is the attribution of subjective function to the objectivisation of a phenomenal or 'functional' centre in each such phenomenon, thereby creating an individual with a suppositious ego-self. In short, the functional focal point of a phenomenal objectivisation has been endowed with a suppositious personal subjectivity whereas its only subjectivity is its noumenality. This suppositional subjectivity is then objectified as an entity possessing full autonomy.

Identification of This-which-we-are with separate phenomenal objects which, without such identification, are simply our phenomenality as such, involves the objectivisation of each. In this process the 'functional' centre comes to be seen as the centre of a suppositional individual with an ego-self, developing thereby a supposed entity where there is merely phenomenality functioning impersonally as subject and object. That is to say, as such it functions subjectively and objectively in split-mind, accompanied by 'space' and 'time', as 'mechanically' as the escapement of a clock.

Absolute-noumenality, manifesting via every sentient being, recognises no entity in the phenomenal cosmos, has no need of such, nor any function that such could fulfil. The existence of an autonomous, volitional entity would be incompatible with the functioning of *prajñā*, and the notion of such seems to be an aberration for which there is no place. An entity, therefore, is 'a dream, an illusion, a bubble and a shadow', as the Buddha said in the Diamond Sutra, a breeze of phantasy that troubles the calm waters of mind without any possibility of effecting anything whatever of a factual character in the dream of phenomenal living.

Note: Yes, yes, quite so. What the Buddha so lucidly, and I so obscurely, have just been describing is—as you suspect—that which you *think* that you are.

26. *Without Tears*

WE MISTAKE the functional centre of the phenomenal aspect of our noumenality for a 'self'. It has no more autonomy than a heart, a physical organ, no more volitional potentialities, and no more self-consciousness; yet we attribute to it the sentience which represents what noumenally we are.

A psyche-soma, phenomenal as it is, must have a functional centre, without which it could not be what is seen as a 'sentient being'. Such centre must be psychic, just as the heart is somatic. The five senses, interpreted by the sixth, depend on this centre for their manifestation as perception and cognition; all functioning, instinctive or rational, is directed therefrom, and it is logical, therefore, that this centre should be considered as the subjective element of the objectivised phenomenon. So, phenomenally, it appears, but itself this 'subject' is an object, so that never could it be what we are, but only a part of the phenomenal set-up of the discriminated and separate phenomenon which we think that we are. Never could it be autonomous, never could it exercise volition, never could *it* be what we conceive as 'us'.

Moreover our sentience is essentially noumenal, and we are mistaking the switch-board for the power-station, the reservoir for the source, an electronic computer for a mind: *the functional centre of a sentient being is purely cybernetic.*

The identification which gives rise to a supposed 'entity' that then and thereby thinks that it is in bondage, is identification of what noumenally we are, of our natural noumenality, with the functional 'organ' in the psyche-soma which becomes thereby a supposed 'self' or 'ego' with relative, if not full, autonomy and volition. We do not even care to remember that only a small fraction of our physical movements, of our organic functioning responds in any way to the initiatives of our personalised wishes.

How does this situation arise? It arises as a result of the splitting of mind, called 'dualism', whereby the phenomenal aspect of noumenality—that is pure impersonal phenomenality—divides into negative and positive, and there appear 'objects' which require a 'subject', and 'others' which require a 'self', each totally dependent on its counterpart for its apparent existence.

But mind, though apparently split in the process of phenomenalisation, remains whole as noumenon, and only in the becoming apparent, or in order to become apparent, is it obliged to divide into an apparent see-er and an apparent seen, a cogniser and a thing cognised, which nevertheless can never be different, never two, for though in function it divides yet in its potentiality it remains whole.

All phenomenality, therefore, is objective, that is appearance in mind, and its appearance is dependent on its division into a see-er or cogniser and what is seen or cognised, that is which becomes apparent to an observer whose existence is assumed in order that appearance may appear. It follows that in all this phenomenality there is no 'ens' anywhere, for neither the apparent cogniser nor the apparently cognised is an entity in its own right, i.e. having a nature of its own, autonomy or volition.

It follows also that the potentiality of 'sentience' whereby all this manifestation is cognised, called *prajnā* in Sanscrit, is an im-mediate expression of noumenality. Utterly impersonal, as devoid of 'ens' as are phenomena, 'it' is nevertheless, and 'it' must necessarily be, what we are, and *all that we are*. In conceptualising 'it' as *prajnā*, 'it' is conceptualising 'itself', via the familiar dualistic process of splitting into conceptualiser and concept or cogniser and cognised, so that in seeking for what we are—that for which we are seeking is the seeker: the seeker is the sought and the sought is the seeker, and that—as Padma Sambhava told us in plain words—*is* what we are.

There is no entity involved anywhere, and space-time here is seen as a conceptual framework which accompanies events in order that events may have the necessary extension whereby they may appear to occur.

Total negation is required, for the Negative Way alone abolishes the factuality of all phenomena and the existence of entity as such, but if a positive representation is to be attempted these are the elements out of which the image seems to be composed.

27. *When the Tail Catches the Kitten*

WHERE IS noumenon?
Ever looked for a spot at the back of your head?

No good!
Ever tried a pain in your 'tummy'?

No good!
Ever thought of a vague nebulosity floating about somewhere or other?

No good!
How difficult you are! What do you suggest?

Too big to be seen at all.
No good!

Why not?
Neither big nor small.

Then let us say that it is ubiquitous?
Ubiquitous means everywhere, and it is nowhere.

How so?
'Where' implies space, and that is only a concept.

Eternal, then.
'Eternal' implies duration in time, which is only a concept.

If it is neither in 'place' nor 'time', it must be here and now.
No good!

Whyever?
In order that there should be a 'here' or a 'there', a 'now', or a 'then', there would have to be some thing that could be here or there, now or then.

And it is no thing?
At last!

So, being no thing, it can have no 'where', no 'when', nor any attribute or qualification whatever.

No statement could be further from the truth of this matter.

Hang it all! What an impossible chap you are! What on Earth *do* you mean?

What made that statement?

I did.

Who is that?

Me.

No such entity anywhere or anywhen.

Well, then, noumenon did.

Quite so, but not perhaps immediately?

You mean via myself?

Via what you are as a phenomenal aspect of noumenon.

Yes, I suppose I am that.

Certainly not! Only 'you' are that.

You mean. . .?

As 'I' you are noumenon, *only a phenomenon can be 'that'.*

I see, I see—But why was my statement wrong?

Because, every phenomenon being the apparent aspect of nou-menon, you have a 'where', a 'when', attributes and qualifications as a phenomenon.

I myself, then, am noumenon?

Certainly not!

Oh dear! Oh dear!! How is that?

As a 'self' you are pure spoof, a not very pretty piece of super-fluous imagination! At most a rumour.

Thanks, old man, but I take it kindly since perhaps you mean it well! I want to get to the bottom of this. Noumenon has attributes in its objective aspect of phenomena or appearance?

There is no such thing as noumenon, which is only a more technical term for 'mind' in its abstract connotation. Noumenon is only cognisable as phenomena.

So that the attributes etc. of phenomena are ultimately the attributes etc. of noumenon?

Strictly speaking—no, but as a concept it may be considered provisionally as a leg-up over a stile.

What, then?

Noumenon is only I, as said by any and every sentient being, for that apparent being's sentience is the 'I' that says it or enables it to be 'said'.

But the phenomenon that actually voices it?

Identical with every other or conceivable phenomenon that was, is, or ever could be.

So that all phenomena are just the appearance of noumenon.

Such is my understanding, at least.

And—even more important—noumenon is just, and only, what appears as phenomena?

What e l s e could it be? 'It' as such is just a concept, surely?

You mean 'it' has no actual existence?

Neither actual nor factual. 'It' is merely 'I'—whoever says it.

And 'I' do not 'exist'?

Quite certainly not; where and when is there for an 'I' to 'exist'? Only 'you's exist.

Yet noumenon, manifesting or appearing as 'phenomena', is ubiquitous in that guise?

You are objectifying it as some 'thing' doing all that.

So what can I say?

'I, "noumenality", manifest or appear as "phenomenality" and I am apparently ubiquitous in that guise'. Neither noumenality nor phenomenality e x i s t s as such, but a r e only in their mutual negation which is fulfilment as I.

Nevertheless every object that my senses perceive, that is every appearance whatever, is only my own noumenality expressed as divers phenomena?

Is only the noumenality which is what you are. . . .

And what I am is all that I perceive and cognise, and all that I perceive and cognise is what I am?

Quite so. Go on.

Go on? Is that not far enough?

Indeed it is not.

What then?

What I am neither is nor is not, and I neither am nor am not as I.

Which 'I' is the absence of the concept of neither is nor is not, neither am nor am not?

Which is as far as words can take it.

So there is nothing further that can be said?

Vimalakīrti's answer was silence when the four bodhisattvas had tried to answer the question as to how they had entered the Dharma-gate of disidentification via apprehending the identity of opposites—the seeker and the sought, self and other, etc. of which this one we have been discussing is the essential.

So that a layman understood more clearly than four bodhisattvas, including Manjusrī?

Quite so, quite quite so; perhaps he understood more deeply— though I am inclined to doubt whether that point, so interesting to us, was the intended climax of the story!

28. *The Only Freedom*

As LONG as there is an 'I' thinking and feeling, no matter how that 'I' may be conceived, that 'I' is an object and is bound—for *all objects*, are necessarily bound.

Even if I should succeed in freeing my 'self' from fear, desire, affectivity of any kind or degree, that freed 'self' is still there as a 'self', and it matters not whether it is freed or not freed from any apparent incubus—for its continued subsistence as a centre that is free or unfree is itself bondage. The fear, desire, affectivity, are manifestations of the pseudo-entity which constitutes bondage; therefore it is the entity, rather than the manifestations thereof, that needs to be eliminated.

An entity must inevitably be bound, for an entity is an object of the subject which it claims to be, and every such object of a subject is in the bondage of apparent causality.

That is why the Masters so often stated that there is no difference between 'enlightenment' and 'ignorance', for *in either condition* there remains a conceptual entity to be the one or the other, to experience the one or the other condition.

Whatever can be stated of a supposed entity or 'self', or 'centre' of any kind, is not different from its opposite, for each is the positive or negative aspect of an inference, an interpretation, which appears to 'exist' and is a concept in mind. Each, whatever it may be, neither is nor is-not, for it is a supposition conditioning an entity which itself is a supposition, so that the condition, or its opposite, or its absence, is a concept applied to a concept, that is the shadow of what is itself a shadow, the substance of which lies in its noumenal origin.

In 'noumenality' alone can there be absence of bondage, for noumenally there cannot be any entity to be bound.

Only noumenal living, therefore, can be free.

29. *What Are We?*

I

WHAT WE are is what I am calling 'whole-mind', which is noumenon. The manifestation of this which we are, is a process of objectivisation entailing a division into two elements—a subject which perceives and an object which is perceived. This is known as 'dualism', and all phenomena, whatever is sensorially perceived, are so constituted, being the correlation of a cogniser and that which is cognised. It is evident that without these two categories nothing could have any kind of phenomenal existence, and it is evident also that neither cogniser nor that which is cognised could have any independent existence, since each only exists in function of the other.

Mind, which we are, therefore, is both its objects, cogniser and cognised; and whatever cognises and is cognised must necessarily exist only in this mind in which this process occurs, and which is what we are.

The cogniser is necessarily what we term 'subject', and that which is cognised is necessarily what we term 'object', and the cognising subject of objects regards his subjective function as constituting an entity which he objectifies as a 'self', i.e. as himself.

This entification enables discrimination to arise, whereby the entified cogniser in order to compare, and so judge, his objects, imagines opposing concepts, such as good and bad, great and small, light and heavy, by means of which he can discriminate between them. This is a further application of the dualistic principle on which phenomenal manifestation entirely depends, and all reasoning is the application of this principle and process.

The mechanism itself of phenomenal manifestation primarily depends on the creation of an imagined objective framework composed of what we know as 'space', in which objects can extend and thereby become apparent, and of what we know as 'time' in which they can have duration, without which their appearance could not be perceived. All phenomenal events depend for their extension or apparent occurrence on these two associated factors together known as 'space-time'.

Such is a schema of the mechanism whereby the so-complex phenomenal universe comes into manifestation and evolves through vast periods of purely suppositional 'time' in a purely suppositional 'space'. Such, also, is what we are, since there is nothing therein that is other than what we are, which is what I have referred to as noumenon or whole-mind.

II

OUR UNHAPPINESS, our so-called 'bondage', all our suffering whatsoever, our 'fall' out of paradise in the Garden of Eden metaphor, is solely the effect of the identification of what we are with the subject or cogniser element of our division into subject and object. The entification of that subject causes a supposedly independent and autonomous individual to be conceived, who can exercise personal volition according to his own good pleasure.

But what we are is neither more nor less the subject-cogniser than the object-cognised, which, as has been pointed out, are entirely interdependent, mutually inseparable in mind, so that neither could possess or exercise any kind of personal volition or independence in any circumstances, since neither could be in any sense an autonomous entity.

It is this illusory entification which constitutes 'bondage', and all suffering whatsoever, for 'bondage' is bondage to that concept. Since, however, the concept is a concept only, there is no entity to be bound, and factually there is not, never has been, and never could be any such thing.

What we are, whole-mind or noumenon, manifested objectively as the totality of phenomena, has no objective existence otherwise than so manifested. Having no objective existence, what we are cannot be subject either to constraint or to liberation, so that our 'bondage' and the suffering dependent thereon, can only have a conceptual basis. Being purely conceptual, that is to say the result of conditioning, we can only be rid of it by understanding profoundly either This-which-we-are or That-which-we-are-not. The former, whether in our noumenal or whole-mind aspect or in our phenomenal or split-mind aspect, we have never ceased to be; the latter, as supposed phenomenal *entities*, we have never been at all, and never could be. Therefore the profound understanding should be recoverable either by apperceiving what we are or by comprehending what we are not, by either or both kinds of cognition.

That can hardly matter, however, since either understanding can only result from the functioning of what we are, and never from the functioning of what we are not, since such functioning is inexistent except as our own functioning misapplied.

In fact the sought which we are is seen as the seeker which we are, the finder as the found, and what is found can only be what we are, since we can never have been anything else. That which we are looking for cannot be anything but this which is looking for itself, but for that very reason it can never be found—for there is nothing to find. What we are is by definition totally devoid of any element of objectivity, what we are is 'looking', is all 'looking', and all 'doing'; it is the Eye which can see everything—but never can hope to see itself.

30. Inbeing

NOUMENALITY IS present wherever and whenever phenomenality is present, for neither can ever have independent existence.

Every phenomenon, at every moment, is then noumenon and is thereby a centre, the centre of an infinity and an eternity of which, since they are by definition without limit, the centre must necessarily be everywhere and always.

That is the only sense in which any phenomenon can be I, and in that limited sense every sentient phenomenon is necessarily I *in every act of sentience*, wherever and whenever such act may occur.

Every sentient appearance can say I, therefore, although itself can never be I *as an appearance.* Consequently noumenally it is I which perform such act wherever and whenever it may be performed and by whatever sentient phenomenon such act may appear to be performed. But neither the (objective) performer of the act nor the (objective) act itself can ever be I, since they are only a phenomenal duality.

That is not easy to say; perhaps it may not be easy to understand, but the inseeing of it is seeing into what we are.

Inseeing, however, is not enough, though its expression reaches the limit of the function of words, for words, being subject to duality, cannot transform inseeing into inbeing—which is disidentification.

31. The Cube-root of Zero

I

MANY ARTICLES and some books have been written about further directions of measurement than the three which are available to our sensory apparatus, and in several European languages. As far as I am aware all are concerned exclusively with what may be called 'the search for an Nth dimension', while higher mathematics, by the use of symbols, can use such suppositional directions of measurement for its own theoretical purposes.

All are searching for something, and these earnest searchers have never found anything. Strange to say, this seems odd to them. Yet the explanation is evident for all to see.

What are directions of measurement? They are measurements from here to there. They can be represented objectively; for instance a line can be drawn from A to B, and that represents length; then a line can be drawn at right-angles to that, from A to B 1, and that represents width, which, together with the former, constitutes a plane surface; then a further line can be drawn, or erected as a model, also at right-angles, from A to B 2, and that represents height, all three directions constituting what is called volume, which is also what we know as 'space'. But all are measurements from A, for A is the centre from which all measurements are made. And what is A? A is the measurer, A is what measures, A is the centre of the universe, A is what we suppose ourselves to be, whoever we are and wherever we are. And since it is A who is now measuring, A is trying to measure itself. That is why there is nothing to be found.

There is no term or description which is adequate for a further direction of measurement, and that for the same reason, i.e. because there is nothing further that is objective to be measured, objectivity being defined by three dimensions only. And no descriptive indication of what is implied has ever been found that is better than that of Jesus—which was simply the word 'within'.

Within what? That is the question. Is there any thing within which a further measurement could be made? What is being searched for is neither behind the beyond nor within the inside, for such are concepts, but just plain here and now. Whether that has been understood or not, it is doubtless the underlying meaning of the tentative definition which declares that 'time is the fourth dimension of space', which is said to have found general acceptance among advanced physicists. Metaphysically we know, as has been explained heretofore, that what we conceive as 'time' is an aspect of what we ourselves appear to be, since without extension in duration phenomena could not be perceived, but multiplying and numbering purely mathematical directions of unimaginable measurement is of technical application only, and has no factual application whatever: it is sufficient to refer to directions of measurement, beyond the three which are sensorially perceptible to us, simply as the Nth dimension.

Since the three directions which are accessible to us describe the universe which is apparent, they are our objective measurements, and no further direction can be such, since our sensory equipment can know no further direction that can be objectified. It follows necessarily that an Nth dimension must be non-objective to us, which is a definition of what noumenally we are. In short it indicates noumenality. The 'kingdom of Heaven' may be a poetic definition, in itself a conceptual objectivisation, but no definition can be otherwise; what it ultimately indicates is our ultimate noumenality.

The searchers have been searching for what was searching, and they have found nothing but mathematical formulae because nothing but mathematical formulae is there to be found, that is to say the most abstract degree of conceptualisation. They were, and no doubt still are, searching for a universe outside the universe which is what they themselves are. In Huang Po's phrase, they are using mind to find mind, and mind cannot find mind any more than an eye can see itself. Noumenon cannot apprehend noumenon otherwise than as phenomena—and here there is none to be apprehended. We are the Nth dimension, which, therefore, is in no direction of measurement from us, and that can not be described, description being objectivisation, because being non-objectivity it cannot objectify itself since it is no thing to be objectified. Every centre of timeless infinity, which in appearance is everywhere and always, can objectify that which is phenomenal, but never can it objectify its own noumenality which is all that it is.

II

Presence

PHENOMENA AND space-time are inseparable: their appearance is interdependent.

Noumenon is non-spatiality and timelessness: the absence itself of all concepts which need extension.

Space-time then is seen as an open gate to metaphysical comprehension.

As long as the concept of space-time is present, only phenomenal comprehension is possible—for only phenomenal comprehension is extended in space and duration.

The absence of the concept of space-time leaves noumenality omnipresent (ubiquitous and eternal), for there is no longer a space or a duration in which anything objective whatsoever can extend.

This abolition, dis-appearance of space-time, then will leave us integrally what we are.

The Great Joke, therefore, is seen to be the apprehension that our suppositional 'bondage' is our dependence on the notion of space-time which alone is responsible for the illusion on which the notion of 'bondage' depends.

Note: Phenomenally, we can know no present, since it must be in the 'past' before our senses can complete the process of recording it, leaving only a suppositional past and future; noumenally there is no question of 'past' or 'future' but only a *presence* which knows neither 'time' nor 'space'.

III

Awakening is waking-up to what is Here

WHY IT IS A JOKE

THE FURTHER or 'Nth' direction of measurement, which indicates where we are, which is Here and Now, is inaccessible alike to sensorial perception and to conceptualisation—the five senses and the conceptualising sixth. We need not doubt the reason for this, which indeed is obvious: it is simply because, being Here and Now, it is itself the centre from which externalisation takes place, and subject cannot objectify itself as subject. Therefore it can only be known in the total absence of conceptualisation.

This is why absence of mentation, of which conation is an element, has been universally recognised as an essential condition of what has been picturesquely termed awakening to 'enlightenment', more accurately 'disidentification'. Conation, or volition, being a direct expression of the subjective, or egotic, aspect of mentation, precludes any possibility of such inseeing—since that is outseeing from a psychic subject which itself is an object and, as such, purely conceptual.

But since we are evidently 'lived'—or 'dreamed' if you prefer—from our common centre in the nearer or Nth dimension, it is from this direction of measurement, our noumenal centre, that all direct, spontaneous and inevitable action or 'God's will', originates, rather than from the phenomenal or pseudo-centre of an egotic subject of conceptualised objects, whose effects are only appearance.

All accounts of direct experience by those who have found their way back—if I may so express it—to their eternal centre, be it called Nirvāna, Dharmakāya, Būtatathatā, Buddha-Mind, True Nature, Self, Tao, Kingdom of Heaven, or anything else, confirm that this noumenal source, or true centre of each and all sentient beings is this tri-dimensionally void I-ness, from which all that is phenomenal originates.

We can deify it if we wish, and term it 'divine' as opposed to 'human', 'Heaven' as opposed to 'Earth', but what it is calls for no devotional or affective approach, which must necessarily conceal it as effectively as an intellectual search. Never could it be 'found'—for what it is, where it is, and when it is, is precisely what, where, and when, the searcher is who is seeking.

Note: It may be desirable to recall that 'space' is here a concept which provides exteriorised objects with the extension necessary to render their appearance 'solid', i.e. perceptible tri-dimensionally as objects, and in spatial relation to other objects, just as 'time' is their equally necessary extension in duration. Time is, therefore, an *extension of space* in duration, and so a further direction of measurement. Space-time as a single concept then utilises four dimensions, three spatial and one temporal.

Space-time, therefore, is an aspect of what phenomenally we appear to be—since it necessarily accompanies our appearance. 'Dimensions', being spatial measurement, i.e. a conceptual analysis of a concept (space or space-time), a further direction, or the 'Nth dimension', although itself no more than a conceptual analysis of what we appear to be, is one that leads us directly and inevitably to the noumenal source of our appearance which is, therefore, what we are and all that we are.

Note: For those concerned with the doctrines of various forms of Buddhism, or as propounded by successive Buddhas, the Nth or inclusive measurement of volume is what is variously described as 'the Void', 'the Middle Way', and 'Dependent Origination'. The first is fairly obvious, but the second is senseless as translated, being neither a 'way' nor in the 'middle' of anything; if conceivable as a 'way' it would need to be described as 'the Inner' or 'the Transcending' Way. The third may be said to find its explanation in super-volume.

32. *The Poor Joke*

BONDAGE IS being dependent, tied up, limited. On, to, by, what? Is it not attachment to a supposed 'will', which is the exercise of personal, independent choice by that supposition with which what-I-am is identified and which is called 'me'?

This merely means that *I use the pronoun 'I' wrongly*. I use it as though this objectivisation here were free to do as 'it' wished, whenever 'it' wished, and wherever 'it' wished. But such a possibility has never arisen, and never could arise: there is no such possibility—for an objectivisation can do nothing of itself, any more than any piece of mechanism can act autonomously.

How has it been possible to *avoid* seeing the absurdity of this notion? It has only been possible by imagining or assuming an invisible, imponderable, untraceable 'entity' which takes charge of this mechanism, like the driver of an automobile, and which refers to the machine and its driver together as 'I' and 'me', identifying itself entirely with the apparatus. Is it difficult to recognise that this assumed personality is factually inexistent, that this supposed 'entity' is just a concept?

This exercise of supposed choice and decision, this series of perpetual acts of will or of wilfulness, called 'volition', is what constitutes bondage, and the ensuing conflict, experienced as suffering, is due to the supposed *need* to act volitionally.

The abandonment of this nonsense must abolish the cause of bondage, bondage being bondage to volition expressed as 'I', and implying the phenomenal object concerned. With the understanding of the incongruity of this notion nothing is left to be bound, and nothing is left that can suffer as 'me'.

For I—as what I am, as *all I am*—am no object. The word 'I' says it. So what is there to be bound, where is there any me-object to suffer, when could there be any conflict and with what?

This assumed 'entity', unidentifiable and an unfounded supposition, acts only as 'volition'. I, as what I am, have none—for I am no object that could have 'volition'. I do not act, there is no actor—for an 'actor' is a concept in mind which could not act as such. What I am is devoid of any trace of objectivity. In short and once again—in no circumstances am I any sort or kind of 'entity'.

What I am is expressed phenomenally as see-ing, hear-ing, feel-ing, taste-ing, smell-ing, think-ing, but there is no objective 'I' that sees, hears, feels, tastes, smells or thinks. How then could I exercise 'volition', choose, decide, accept, refuse, or play the clown in any such phenomenal performance?

Objects 'live' sensorially or are 'lived' sensorially, and what I am is their sentience. If I so function, objects live as they must—and there is no need for the notions of bondage, conflict, or suffering—since I do not, and can not, exercise 'volition' which alone is responsible for these.

What absurd clowns 'we' are whose joke is to 'want', to 'wish', to 'desire', 'hope', 'regret'! No wonder clowns are notoriously tragic figures at heart!

33. *The Dungeon*

THE ILLUSION of separateness is due to the apparent presence of objects whose cogniser is their suppositional subject.

Separateness is itself the essential condition on which the notion of bondage depends, and its dissolution entrains the abolition of the idea of being bound.

But the suppositional subject is itself an object, whose cogniser is the nature itself of cognition, so that cogniser and all that is cognised are an inseparable totality in Bhutatathatā or Whole-mind.

Recognition of wholeness leaves no centre to which a notion of separateness could be attached, so that universal identity alone can subsist.

Such recognition is perfect liberation from solitary confinement in the prison of self.

34. Here and Now

'THERE IS neither destiny nor free-will,
  Neither path nor achievement; *this is the final truth*'.

(Stray Verses) p. 93

Maharshi's statement specifically negates the concepts themselves, and the applicaton of them only by inference.

'Destiny', like 'free-will', is a word which seeks to describe a concept, as also are 'path' and 'achievement'. They are not sensorial perceptions, interpreted as having objective existence, but structures in mind whose existence is inferential only, i.e. directly conceptual.

Therefore they cannot have any nature of their own, such nature as pertains to them depending entirely on an assumed 'entity' to which they as concepts can be applied. Being nothing themselves, their truth or falsehood depends upon the truth or falsehood of the 'entity' to which they are attached and whose comportment they are designed to explain.

It follows that if there is an 'entity', a question arises as to whether such entity suffers 'destiny' or not, exercises 'free-will' or not, has a 'path' to follow or not, can claim an 'achievement' or not.

There seem to be two ways of answering this question: one is by asking the awakened Masters, the other is by asking oneself. As for the former I think I am correct in stating that in all Advaïta, whether Vedantic or Buddhic, the totality of great and known Masters have categorically declared that no such thing as an entity has ever existed, exists or ever could exist. The Buddha mentions the fact nineteen times in the short Diamond Sutra alone.

As for ourselves, each of us can try to locate such an entity either subjectively or objectively. The results of my own efforts, if that should have any interest, have been entirely, and in my view definitively, negative. So that it seems to me to be reasonable to declare that the explanation of Maharshi's magnificently categorical statement is that there is neither an entity to suffer destiny, nor an entity to exercise free-will, neither an entity to follow a path, nor an entity to achieve an aim.

Should it not follow that if we are lived, without attempted 'volition' on the part of a purely suppositional 'entity', we may ask what could there be to have cares and worries, for the disappearance of a supposed 'path' can only leave what inevitably must be our normal and eternal condition here and now, in lieu of 'achievement'?

Note: An entity requires inferences such as 'space' and 'duration', an entity is subject to limitation, an entity is an object and needs a subject.

35. The Essential Query

WHERE AM I?
I am where no things are not.

That is to say:
I am where things, which are not in fact 'things', and so are no things—are not.

This is the double negative of Shen Hui as clearly as it can be expressed in words.

Let us say it with a pronoun:
What am I?
I am what no thing is not.

That is to say:
I am what any thing, which is never in fact a 'thing', and so is no thing—is not.

I do not know whether it may be possible to point more directly at what we are.

Note: Of course instead of the general word 'thing' we can say 'object', '*dharma*', 'phenomenon': all describe the constituents of the conceptual universe in which all phenomena appear.

In this simple statement, in common terms, subject and object, noumenon and phenomena, are no longer separate: what I am is whatever each is and whatever both are when they are not either.

36. *Abolition of Opposites*

ALL OPPOSITES are the voidness of mind which is what we are—cognised as such when apperceived as void of opposition.

'Voidness of mind' is what remains when mind is voided of mind.

We cannot apperceive opposites as not-different without *at the same time* seeing them as different, why and how they are fundamentally and eternally different as phenomena. Their *essential* phenomenal separation or division-into-two itself constitutes their inseparability and indivisability noumenally, just as, or because the separation of phenomena themselves conceptually from noumenon, is the very expression of their ultimate or non-conceptual identity.

All are just the absence of non-conceptuality; that is to say that they are what every concept is, which in fact as a concept is not any 'thing', so, being no 'thing', thereby is not at all.

Opposites themselves are not different from their composites, when conceivable, for the same reason, i.e. because they both are what any thing, which is never in fact a 'thing', and so is no-thing, is not.

Ethical and Affective Opposites

No action can be either 'right' or 'wrong', because there is no such thing as volitional 'action'; and non-volitional action, being inevitable, cannot be qualified at all. Therefore there cannot be any thing that can be qualified as either, and neither has any existence other than as an arbitrary judgment without factual basis.

'Liking' and 'disliking', also, are affective reactions on the part of a pseudo-entity which as such has only a conceptual existence. Being relative expressions of an inference, they have no validity whatever, either as such or in their more developed expressions as 'love' and 'hate'. Their difference, then, is only apparent.

All adjectives are void, because no noun to which they can be attached has any existence except as a concept. Therefore the difference of each from its opposite can only be a phenomenal interpretation.

'Result' and 'method' are one, which means that neither is cause or effect of the other; 'methods' may follow 'results' in a time-sequence, which is to say that they may appear to result from 'results', and vice-versa, but they are opposing manifestations devoid of difference except as appearance. They offer a ready means of apperceiving that cause/effect also are not separate in origin.

This applies also to 'difference' and 'identity' (as non-difference), which should dispose of the 'opposites'—which are neither different nor identical (as non-different); and also the seeing of this mutual voidness and the non-seeing of it (as not being conscious of not seeing it), for all are simultaneous apperceptions and at the same time spontaneous.

37. *Essential Definition*

Subject and object are the dual objective faces of what subjectively they are—sometimes absurdly and misleadingly described as the 'Middle Way'.

What subjectively they are can only be known as Void because the knowing of that is an attempted objectivisation of what-they-are, whereby nothing can be cognised—since what is cognising cannot cognise itself.

Void, however, is not such—for it is I. What they are is what we are and what, for every sentient being, is what I am.

And I am the presence of the absence of all that seems to be.

Comment

This formulation applies to all pairs of 'opposites', for instance all that is conceived as 'obverse or reverse', 'heads or tails', 'front or back', 'here or there', 'this or that', *'pile ou face'*. Phenomenally regarded, they are mutually exclusive alternatives, one *or* the other.

'Self *or* other', 'noumenon *or* phenomenon' are not different, since all as such are objects—even 'subject' and 'noumenon'—conceptually regarded. But if 'and' is substituted for 'or', or if the nouns are hyphenated, as 'subject-object', each pair is then being regarded as one single object—which they can never be *positively* but only as a result of their mutual *negation*, which requires not 'and' but 'neither . . . nor . . .'

Always 'noumenon or phenomena' are the essential pair of opposites, for the one implies the source of all that could be, and the other defines every thing that could appear. They are, therefore, all-inclusive.

Regarded objectively, which is equivalent to being regarded at all, they are the negative and positive faces of what subjectively they are—like any other pair of 'contraries', since both are then being objectified. Thus what they are is their mutual negation or the absence of no-phenomena.

But they are then and also what we are, what each of us is as 'I'. Phenomena are what we appear to be as a result of an interpretation of sensorial perception, and noumenon is what each of us is antecedent to this perceptive-conceptive process, manifested and unmanifested respectively.

This, of course, only can be suggested by the personal pronoun 'I'. But whereas, on the one hand, 'I' as a noun implies either noumenality or phenomenality, on the other, as a pronoun, it implies neither the one nor the other; devoid of any qualification soever, it implies the origin of the origin of phenomena, the origin of this by which phenomena are manifest, and in which both entirely inhere in subjectivisation.

No word, or form of words, no sound or symbol could ever indicate the meaning of 'I', which Maharshi called 'I–I', but even this Sanscrit locution, though it could hardly be bettered, is inadmissible. Why? Simply because the mere attempt to express, and so objectify it, is turning away from what it is—which is also the turning that is turning away from what is turning away from what is turning.

38. Thought: What is it?

ALL THOUGHT is objectification,
Of what? Of what I am.
I can, therefore, objectify what I am?

Acting via an intermediate object from moment to
moment as intermediate subject, that is as 'phenomenal
subject', such thought cannot objectivise, or constitute an
objectivisation of, what-I-am, since what I am is what
thought is: and mediate thought as such cannot think itself.

'Direct thought' Shen Hui termed 'absolute thought',
sometimes translated 'thought of the Absolute'. Living
according to absolute thought is direct living, what I have
termed 'non-volitional living', or *wu wei*, as the Masters
lived.

Living according to mediate (indirect) thought is the
life of men who mistake the mediate subject for an entity,
because it appears to act, and identify themselves with that,
thereby finding that they are in suppositional bondage.
Mediate thought objectivises everything, for objectivisation
is its function and what it is; it objectivises every thing
except itself which is no thing, and that—which is *This*,
or direct thought—it cannot objectify.

But direct—or absolute—thought is the process of
objectivisation of what-I-am, which is what we are as sentient
beings, which constitutes the apparent universe and maintains
it in the apparent seriality which is the temporal aspect of
space-time. It can have no other objectivisation of itself than
this apparent universe, for it cannot objectivise itself, either
directly or mediately otherwise than as phenomena, since
itself as such has no objective quality to be perceived as an
object. Attempts at self-objectivisation via a mediate subject
therefore can only arrive at the percept of emptiness,
conceptualised as 'the Void', since what is perceived is void
of all objects—which is then the objective appearance of
what-I-am. Phenomenally, therefore, what I am, what all
sentient beings are subjectively, is voidness of objectivity;
utterly non-objective, what we are is the imperceptible
source of everything, itself inexistent as a 'thing'.

Suggestions by the qualified concerning its nature never exceed notions such as 'light', 'colour', 'bliss', 'infinite awareness', in Sanscrit '*sat-chit-ānanda*', implying ineffable self-consciousness devoid of 'form', 'force', 'character', or any quality soever. 'I' might be illustrated conceptually as 'unlimited potentiality', non-manifesting *Dhyāna* becoming manifest via *Prajnā*, its cognising expression, which as 'thought' is the subject of these observations.

When mediate thought is quiescent immediate thought remains, ubiquitous and eternal, and such *is* what I am, but it could never describe what it is, since itself would then be the describing of what is describing what is being described.

An immediate thought, which is non-conceptual and so non-dual—unsplit into subject and object—itself being what is, can know no bondage.

39. *Wu Nien* 無念

IT SHOULD make no difference whether we dispose of 'self' or 'other', for the disposal of either eliminates both.

The method proposed by the Masters is to 'cease thinking', for then neither 'self' nor 'other' exists any longer. The expression 'to cease thinking' means to cease thinking *as from a self*, for pure thought, 'absolute thought', 'direct thought', 'the one thought' (non-dualist thought), *wu nien*, is what thought is when there is no thinker.

Wu Wei 無爲

TO LIVE totally is to cease living partially—as we usually do, that is not to 'live' more, but to 'live' less, these two adverbs denoting volitional living.

By ceasing to live volitionally we necessarily live totally—which is *wu wei*.

Living totally there can no longer be conflict between the noumenality which we are and a conceptual 'entity', which appears as a 'self', and which produces anguish and the sensation of bondage.

Living in totality implies that our phenomenality inheres integrally in noumenon which, in Buddhist terminology, represents undifferentiated *samsāra* and *nirvāna*.

40. *Bewildering Bits and Painful Pieces. II*

LEAVE OBJECTS to look after themselves, if any, and recognise the absence of their subject as an object.

❧   ❧   ❧

'Non-abiding' means not abiding in a 'self'.

❧   ❧   ❧

That which is self is other: that which is other is self,
And this which I am is neither self nor other.

❧   ❧   ❧

Dialectic mind, divided into subject and object, reasoning by means of the comparison of opposites, necessarily sees such opposites, all opposites, as different.
But whole-mind, noumenon, equally necessarily, sees them as not different.
Rather simple, quite obvious? Surely.

❧   ❧   ❧

Each 'other' becomes (or is) a 'self' to itself, and each 'self' becomes (or is) an 'other' to another 'self'. This is what 'individuals' are.

❧   ❧   ❧

'Jesus said to them: "When you make the two one . . . then you will go into the Kingdom." Gospel of Thomas.'

❧   ❧   ❧

The resolution of opposites is their coincidence in mutual negation.

❧   ❧   ❧

Functioning and potentiality, cognisable as the Functioning of Potentiality, are Prajñā the Seeker, Dhyāna the Sought. Finding the seeker is finding the sought. 'We' are

the seeker, the see-er, the perceiver, the cogniser, 'we' are
Prajnā. 'We' are the sought, seen, the perceived, the cognised,
we are *Dhyāna*. And their absence as *Prajnā-Dhyāna* is what
we are.

❖   ❖   ❖

The interdependent counterpart of 'phenomenal' is
not 'noumenal' but 'non-phenomenal'. 'Noumenal' is the
absence of 'non-phenomenal.'

❖   ❖   ❖

Homage

He is a better dog than I am a man, and sometimes
a better man also.

I do not pat him, I bow to him.

I called him my dog, now I wonder if I am not his
man?

❖   ❖   ❖

The void must be void, also, of voidness.

❖   ❖   ❖

You? You—whoever you may be—are just an error
of perception or a misinterpretation of the facts.

❖   ❖   ❖

Non-Objective Relation

My absence as 'me' is my presence as God, and 'your'
absence as my object is 'your' presence as God, so that our
mutual absence as 'us' (subject and object) is our mutual
presence as God. Which is non-objective relation.

❖   ❖   ❖

Another droll activity is attempting to do away with,
or escape from, a 'self'. How can a shadow eliminate itself?

The shadow will disappear the moment its substance
is no longer seen as such, for there will then be nothing to
cast a shadow.

What is the use of noughting yourself?
Who is noughting who?
What is the use of searching for yourself?
Who is searching for who?
There are not two of you!

You cannot find yourself, or the absence of yourself.
You are yourself, but you don't know what you are, and
Your guess is wrong!

❖   ❖   ❖

I think that I act; an 'I' acts me,
But all the time I am being dreamed by what-I-am.

❖   ❖   ❖

The 'apparent' and the 'real' are not different. Why
is that? Because they are both words for what our senses
propose.

❖   ❖   ❖

Definition

Subject is in fact *total object*. As total objectivity it is
total subjectivity. 'It' is neither either nor both, but can be
conceived as abstract totality. Called 'subject', it is an object;
called 'object', it is subject. In their mutual negation it
remains as I.

❖   ❖   ❖

Negation is Acceptance

Negation implies acceptance, because it is the self-
nature or autonomous existence of phenomenal objects that
is being denied, and this comports acceptance of these same
phenomenal objects, as appearances, so that resistance to
them disappears, and they are accepted as manifesting what
we are.

PART III

NON-OBJECTIVE RELATION

I dream the Universe
And all that I dream is I,
I who am not.

I dream the Universe,
And you perceive it.

41. *Thought as Action*

ACTION IS a demonstration of thought.
Action, being the exterioration of thought,
Dualistic thought demonstrates as volitional action.

Action that is the exterioration of thought is volitional action. Such thought, and its demonstration in action, are effects of split-mind and they confirm bondage.

'Pure' thought is reflected in 'pure' action.

'Pure' thought *(wu nien)* and non-volitional action *(wu wei)* are directly noumenal. Their apparent difference is phenomenal.

42. 'Reincarnation' Again

THE LOW-DOWN on 'reincarnation' is just that I never was 'born' and could not possibly 'die'. So what? So of course the chap who is convinced he was Julius Caesar, and the girl who 'remembers' she was Cleopatra; each and all and every one of them, are right. So indeed they were.

Why? Because so was I, of course, bald as an egg and with a lovely nose (respectively).

What is there, what could there be, to be born or to die—except hair and noses—anyway?

So I have always been alive and never dead? Good Heavens, No! The reason is that I have never been alive and so I can never be dead.

That is the final truth concerning 'reincarnation'. (If you don't see it now—patience, you will.)

43. Non-Objective Relation

PEOPLE DECLARE that 'self' and 'other' must be seen as 'one' in order that disidentification may take place.
'Self' can never be 'other', and 'other' can never be 'self'.

Because split-mind can never see opposites as one?
That is not the basic reason.

Because a psyche cannot hold two concepts at the same time?
Also true, but still not the basic reason.

Why, then?
Because they never were, are not, and never will be two.

They are basically one?
Nor one either. 'Not-two', advaita, is not 'one'.

Then what is it?
It is neither . . . nor. . . .

As that, then, what is it?
That which is two in objectivity, conceptualised, unconceptualised is an absence whose opposing elements are no longer different but also are not 'one'.

So that phenomenally we, you and I, are mutually 'self' and 'other', but noumenally are not different although not 'one' being?
Exactly.

Why is that so?
Because 'self' and 'other' combined do not constitute a third 'self'.

A 'self' or 'being' is purely phenomenal?
And therefore merely conceptual.

Then non-objective relation, which can occasionally be recognised for a flash, does not indicate unity?
Nor does it admit diversity.

Why can that flash of non-objective relation never be held?
'Holding' implies duration, and non-objective relation is intemporal.

There is no means of conserving it?
Not as long as you allow split-mind—which is only a reflection —to attempt to make a positive, a unity, of a duality. How could it have duration? Duration is the 'lasting' of objects.

Then whole-mind can hold it indefinitely?
Whole-mind can o n l y hold it indefinitely: it knows nothing of 'time'.

But can I hold our unity indefinitely?
No, because there never was 'unity' even for a 'flash'.

Then can I hold our 'non-difference' indefinitely?
Not as long as there is a 'you' to hold it.

In order to know and to hold our non-difference I must cease to be?
You must cease to be as 'you', but you remain as 'I'. And then you a r e our non-difference.

As 'I', I can hold our non-difference indefinitely?
As 'I', you already hold our non-difference eternally.

So I only have to know myself as 'I'?
You cannot know y o u r s e l f as 'I'—because 'I' is not a thing that can be known.

But the Masters knew it!
And you know it—as 'I', but not as your self.

To know that I know it as 'I' is awakened living? As the Masters lived?
As we all can live. If we know that we are already awake.

Then non-objective relation is normal to the awakened?
It is inevitable, for no sentient being has ever been 'asleep'.

44. *La Vida Es Sueño*

THERE IS *one* dream
And no dreamer.
This-which-we-are is the dreaming,
And each of us is dreamed.

Each of us dreams also but our dreams are personal
to each,
And our apparent self is always the centre of our
dream.

I dream the universe,
And all that I dream is I,
I who am, but am not as I,
I dream the universe—and you perceive it,
You who are not, but who are as I.

Note: This is not just pseudo-poesy. The greatest Masters, including
the Buddha, said it and meant it—*literally.*

The object is dreamed; all appearances are just
dreamed.
But the conceptual interpretation of perception, and
perception itself, take place via dreamed objects. That is
the function of sensorialised phenomena.

As objects they are dreamed, but they are essentially
organs of interpretation by whose interpretive functioning
the universe appears. Thus all is dreamed by sentient 'beings'
though their own dreams are personal microcosmic repro-
ductions or second-degree examples of the dream which their
own living constitutes. Essentially both kinds of dream are
identical, as whatever Buddha gave us the Diamond Sutra
implied, and so many Masters confirmed, none more categorically than Vasishta, who stated that there was no
difference whatever between the two categories of dreaming
—the one which each of us dreams nightly and the other in
which all of us are 'lived'.

All, therefore, that we know, or can ever cognise, is
in mind—as the Lankavatāra and other Sutras, and so many
great Masters explicitly, and all the great Masters implicitly,
declared.

That, in fact, is the ultimate burden of Buddhist teaching, as it is of the Diamond Sutra and the Mahā Ramayāna, and the esoteric basis underlying all the greater religions, and no doubt the lesser ones also, with the difference that in the simpler and dualistic ones the Dreamer is entified and made personal as 'God', whereas in the *Advaita*, or non-dual faiths the dreamer is recognised as what-we-are; but those who awaken in the dualist faiths always recognise their ultimate identity with their Deity when such awakening occurs.

❖   ❖   ❖

Just to say that we are dreamed would be misleading, for we are both dreamed and dreaming. This is the essential element in the understanding of what we are. There is not any dream*er*, 'divine' or 'human', or any *thing* dreamed: that is axiomatic, but there is the actual current dreaming of phenomenality, and the apparent universe so dreamed is composed of the mind which is dreaming it, so that every dream-figure is part of the dreaming and is not merely an object being objectivised or dreamed; each object dreamed is also itself the dreaming, in its subjective as in its objective aspect, which comprise the dualistic mechanism of the appearance of the dream, somewhat as the 'escapement' mechanism of a clock alternately releases and arrests its functioning in Time.

To say that 'Life's a dream' is to say everything that a popular phrase could express. The word 'dream' is an image, not a technical term, but it is also more than an image, for what our 'living' activity represents is not different from what our 'sleeping' activity represents; all the same factors are present and in operation, and what is 'produced', what appears in each case, is identical in kind as in origin.

Just as 'we' are every object in *our* 'personal' dreams, so what-we-are is every object in our 'living' dream, no matter how diverse or opposed their activities may appear—for, as we know so well, 'opposites' are merely dual aspects of what subjectively is not divided, although at the same time 'that' does not exist at all as one 'thing', for it has not then any objective existence, and in objectivisation, or becoming apparent, it manifests in two apparently opposing aspects.

Action, true action, therefore, is both dreamed and dream-ing, lived and liv-ing, for there is neither dreamer nor dreamed, God nor man, Creator nor creature. That is why it is called 'non-action', *wu wei*, for no entity performs it, nor is any thing performed, and its 'spontaneity' or 'instance' is all that it can be said to be; it, too, is just an act-ing.

I think that I act; in fact I act 'me': all the time 'I' am being dreamed by what I am. Those are three degrees of understanding and incomplete for, since I am being dreamed by what I am, I am the dreaming both of my action and of the actor of the action, so that I am the *acting* of the action, which is all that can be said to be.

If you are asleep, it cannot be you who dream: if you are 'dreamed', who is dreaming? That which is sleeping cannot be dreaming for, the one being passive and the other active, the two conditions are incompatible simultaneously. That which is passive (sleeping) might be dreamed by that which is active, but then that which is active would be the dreamer and he cannot be dreamed.

Sleep implies cessation of functioning, but if there were a dreamer of dreams such dreamer would necessarily be awake in order to perform the function of dreaming.

All degrees and kinds of dreaming are phenomenal and represent a functioning of mind which, in order to dream, must be awake. Absence of such functioning must result in absence of dreaming, which is called 'deep sleep'.

The dreaming function, therefore, must always be awake. What can it be called except *Prajñā*?

45. *My Dear Fellow!*

IF SUBJECT objectifies or ceases to objectify, then he must be objectif*iable*, for he *is* some thing that *does* some *thing*?

But when he ceases objectifying he has no object, and then can no longer be *subject*. The phrase '*Pure* Subject', still indicates an object. But he is not, and never has been, and never could be, an object, so he is not, never has been, never could be a subject or Subject, pure or impure.

He is not any thing: he is not 'he'. He is I! No thing, just I. Neither pure nor impure: just I.

Objectifying this I, which is all that I am, is the height of absurdity—and the cause of all the trouble in the Universe, in the Cosmos: it is trouble itself as such.

Looking for it, for me, is clowning or lunacy: there has never been any such monstrosity: it is phantasmagoric. The notion is not even thinkable; it is *totally inconceivable*.

A billion objects may be conceived, and each of them may be called 'me', or mis-taken for 'me', but not one could ever be 'me', nor all of them either. Why? If there could be such a thing as a 'me' it would need 'a' subject—and I could not possibly have one! How could I have a subject when I am I? Such 'a' subject would then be an object—and I could no longer be what I am, i.e. I!

You see what utter nonsense such a supposition *must necessarily* be? Fancy anybody searching for 'me'! Who could be such a fool? Some poor chap in a loony-bin? Never, those poor fellows—or are they?—are far too sane!

For Heaven's sake take care not to be caught in such a simple and obvious intellectual booby-trap as to let yourself think for one moment that I could be either subject or object! And whatever for? Am I not I? What more could I be? What more could you want? What else is there, could there be—to want or to be? Heavens above, is it not enough to be I? Nothing else IS!

Note: Is a Buddha uttering this platitude, or is a beetle? Yes, that is why searching can only lead to finding that the sought is the seeker—and the seeker is the sought. But Padma Sambhava says that is enough, and who could know better? A Buddha, a beetle?

46. Self-naughting

SOME EARNEST searchers even come to expressing the desire to abolish themselves.
Impossible. No object can do that.

Suicide?
That is subject killing object: murder.

Why can one not abolish oneself?
There is only one 'one'—who is not 'one' at all.

So what is to do?
Be what you are, and cease pretending to be what you are not.

Sounds easy, but is it?
As long as there is no fatuous 'volition' concerned—yes. It does not need any doing.

How so?
It is not any kind of doing.

It is not-doing?
Not just not-doing, but the absence of not-doing.

Why?
Not-doing is a kind of doing like any other, and that kind too must not be done.

Doesn't sound easy to me!
It is neither difficult nor easy: neither term is applicable. It is not anything qualifiable, because it is not any kind of action at all.

Then what is it?
Just plain being what you are, always were, and will be forever.

Then why cannot my volition achieve it?
Because 'your volition' is a very precise definition of what you are not, and a very sufficient explanation of why you are prevented from living, instead, as what you are.

Which is a way of saying that it prevents me from attaining enlightenment?

It is a way of talking sense, not nonsense! You have no 'me' to be prevented from anything, you could not possibly have anything to 'attain', and there has never been any such 'thing' or 'experience' or 'state' as 'enlightenment' to be 'attained' by anybody or nobody!

My conclusion appears to have been somewhat—shall we say—unfortunate!

Not unfortunate—just plain idiotic! Try again.

What you said about volition was perhaps a way of saying that the 'exercise' of supposed free-will is in fact a direct manifestation of what I am not?

That is so. When you know that you can do nothing directly, when 'free-will' is latent or absent, then what you are remains present and potentially patent.

47. *Identity. II*

Sine Qua Non

As LONG as you are present (or I am) what we are cannot be not-absent.

Whenever you are absent (or I am) what we both are cannot be not-present.

That is why any procedure, method, practice, technique, involving egotic presence, must inevitably defeat its own purpose, for purpose itself is egotic manifestation.

Your (or my) absence is only possible as a result of complete dis-appearance (de-phenomenalisation) of consciousness of identity, and the only evident method of rendering that possible should be the absolute comprehension, based on analytical conviction, that no such identity could possibly exist otherwise than as an illusory concept.

Profoundly apperceiving the nature of this conditioned misapprehension may open the way to awareness and disidentification. Psychically so de-conditioned, an adventitious circumstance may bring about our disappearance as identities, and that absence will leave you (or me) as all that we are.

Note: 'You', 'I', 'me' and 'our' are used here in a purely conventional manner, i.e. as apparent and supposed identities.

❖   ❖   ❖

You can never find your Self via an object of your Self.

You cannot use self to find Self, because the Sought that is searching for itself cannot find itself by means of what is not there.

I could never find Myself via an object of Myself, via a phenomenal objectivisation of Myself.

But I am not searching for Myself, I should have no need even if there were an 'I' to seek or a 'Me' to be sought. There is a searching on the part of, on behalf of, an appearance that is deluded into thinking that it is 'a' noumenon—as though any such absurdity, any such contradiction in terms, could be!

This-which-is-the-'searcher' is necessarily noumenon, or rather the 'searching' is noumenal, pertaining to noumen-ality, that is whatever we phenomenally, with divided minds, imagine dualistically as such. But there is no entity anywhere in the performance.

❖   ❖   ❖

They cannot find their Self via their self, not so much because there is no (objective) 'Self' to find and no (objective) 'self' to search, as because *there is no* (subjective or objective) *'they' to do anything whatever.*

Does that statement not throw you directly into the arms of what you are? Or leave you naked, revealed to yourself as your own total absence as 'self'?

No, it *doesn't*? Well, then, that is just because you are what you are, and only what you are, already! *Here* and *Now:* you are what *'doesn't'*.

48. Gravity

Has any man of science ever calculated how much of our energy is expended daily, or hourly, in struggling to oppose gravitational pull? Life, every moment of life, seems to be accompanied by this incessant struggle to defeat gravity. Is gravity not our supreme foe? Is not gravity the source of the major part of our misery, the unrelenting scourge which makes a burden of our lives? Is it not itself a definition of 'burden'? Is it not the source and origin of the very idea of 'weight'? Does not whatever 'weighs' on our minds take its sense of suffering from the unrelenting example of gravity, without which it could not know 'weight'?

Freed from the burden of 'gravity', should we not dance—not only in body, but also in mind?

But since we cannot free our bodies from the all-embracing physical *emprise* of this our everlasting tormentor, may we not nevertheless free our minds, over which the power of our apparent enemy must be ineffectual? In order to do that we have one way, and one way only: *we* cannot free *our* minds, any more than we can free *our* bodies. What we can do, and all we can do, is to free both our minds and our bodies of our 'selves', without which gravity would remain as powerless over us as it is powerless over a shadow, for without 'us' a concept of 'weight' cannot any longer have anything on which to weigh or to make any impression whatever.

Note: Perhaps the somatic apparatus cannot be so freed, except in trance, but in itself it does not 'suffer' from the incidence of gravity, to which it is adjusted. It is the *conceptual* 'we' that suffers and can be abandoned.

49. *Mr and Mrs Space-time*

WE COULD not cognise volume (three directions of measurement) if we were not looking from a fourth, for it is only from a superior dimension that all inferior dimensions can be perceived.

This also is because what-we-are must necessarily be the further dimension, superior to those which we are able to perceive, since it is only from the second that the first can be perceived, the first and second (plane surface) from the third, and the first, second and third (or volume) from a fourth.

Since we ourselves, then, are regarding the three from a fourth direction, must it not be from the dimension termed 'duration' that we are looking?

If that should be so, then what we call 'Time', which also occupies that position, as the durational dimension of space, may be our name for what we are, as 'Space' may be our name for 'where' we are, and 'Space-time' our proper denomination.

50. *Ostriches, all Ostriches . . .*

WHO THINKS he has a 'self'?
Who thinks he h a s any thing?

Well, who?
Must it not be another 'self'?

Then who is that other 'self'?
'Who?'

Yes, but who is 'who'?
Just who. Who else could it be?

You require a lot of patience!
Y o u ask a lot of stupid questions!

Why are they stupid?
Because such answer as there may be is as available to you as it is to me.

'Who?' can only be yet another 'self'.
Evidently. And who is that yet-another-self?

All I can say is that there must be still another 'self' to know of that one!
Evidently!

But that can go on forever!
It is commonly known as 'a perpetual regression'.

But that is considered a bad thing?
It is considered an absurdity, logically a definition of something that is impossible.

So that an *e n d l e s s* series of 'selves' is impossible?
Evidently: quite meaningless.

Except the first that we are told to get rid of?

The first is no different from the last: if there is no last, then there can be no first either.

Because since there can be no last there can be no second to know a first, and so on forever? Then the first is meaningless?

Quite.

Then why are we required to get rid of it?

We aren't: it was never there. You have just proved it to your own satisfaction!

Then it is the idea that we are required to get rid of?

That is so.

But an idea that is so demonstrably nonsensical hardly needs to be got rid of?

If you know that it couldn't be there, you must be a pretty big ass if you need to get rid of it!

And yet the world is chock-full of such big asses?

That can be explained, but may not so easily be excused!

How do people avoid seeing it?

By concluding that the regression is impossible, and shutting their eyes to the reason why.

They still adhere to the notion of 'self' and pretend that it can exist without being subject to regression?

That seems to be so.

But such a proceeding is absurd?

Ostriches are said to think it a good idea!

But can the idea be admissible and the negation still be valid? or v i c e - v e r s a ?

That would imply that it is the reasoning that is false whereas the premise is unattackable.

Whereas the reasoning is patently unattackable and the premise is demonstrably false.

That is so. If such a proceeding could be admitted no reasoning could be valid, and the totality of science and philosophy, applied as well as theoretical, would become valueless at once.

People are conditioned from babyhood to take this notion of 'self' for granted?

No doubt. Also it seems, very superficially, to fit in with an inherent instinct that all sentient beings must have.

Which instinct?

Because phenomena are only appearances, as the word defines them, it does not follow that they have no apparent centre.

Every living appearance must have a centre?

Every dreamed appearance also must have a dreamed centre. Every apparent body must have an apparent heart.

And for protection it must know 'fear'?

So one may conclude.

And in order to know 'fear' there must appear to be a 'self' to be so protected?

That seems reasonable to me.

So that from that moment a purely suppositional 'self' is assumed?

And the assumption sticks.

Until someone like you points out that its existence is entirely impossible!

Why drag me into it? Even the Buddha was not the first to notice that! Probably it has been axiomatic since the beginning of time.

And all the Masters that ever were, and ever will be, teach it! But why, since it is so obvious, have they made it so complicated?

It seems to be a kind of axiom that what is obvious does not appear to be so to the conditioned mind.

Why should that be so?

Intuitionally it is obvious, but intuition is unconditioned. Logically it is obvious, but conditioning is more powerful than reasoning.

So what are we required to do?

If you see it intuitionally—believe it! If you cannot so see it, then see it logically—and believe it!

How can I help believing it?

My poor, dear fellow, you cannot! You h a v e seen it. Is not that enough?

51. Kittens, all Kittens . . .

WHAT WE were saying about the perpetual regression of the notion of 'self' should also be applicable to the notion of 'subject'?

What applies to 'self and other' applies equally to 'subject and object'. Just as 'other' must have a 'self' which regresses perpetually, so 'object' must have a 'subject', which, becoming an object in order to be, or exist, as a subject, requires another 'subject' and regresses forever.

Anything more important that can be disposed of like that?

What could be more important than subject/object? Don't they take everything else with them?

Cause/effect for example?

Every effect must have a cause, so where does a cause come from?

I haven't an idea!

Do you think it emerges from the thigh of Jupiter or rises like Venus from the sea?

Mildly improbable. You mean it is an effect?

It is as much an effect as it is a cause.

So that it, too, must have a cause that is an effect?

Clearly: no one could dispute it.

And so on for ever and ever—until the cows come home?

Until before the cows ever came out.

Which implies that since a perpetual regression requires the inexistence of that which regresses, just as there cannot be such a 'thing' as a subject or an object, a self or an other, so there cannot be such 'things' as cause and effect?

Surely we all know that already, so that it is a platitude? We are merely proving it logically, so why make such a fuss about it?

Proving it logically seems to me to imply burying it once and for all.

Buried things merely decay: we are cremating it and throwing the ashes to the four winds of heaven.

But if there is no 'first cause' how does manifestation arise?

From non-manifestation.

But how?

By means of three spatial dimensions and a fourth that is cognised as duration.

So cognised, all phenomena can appear, and are taken as real?

They a r e real: they appear as things: 'real' means 'things', and that is what appears.

So that phenomena are reality?

Of course. How could there be any other? Must you ask such stupid questions?

Sorry, but people have been known to use the word 'reality' for noumenality.

Noumenality, not being objectivisable, cannot be a 'thing'. Because people talk nonsense—must you do so also?

But this manifestation business?

A bore, I know well; nevertheless it seems to occur, doesn't it?

But why does it occur?

I seem to remember the Buddha being up against that point.

And what solution did he propose?

Subject to correction, I think he told people to mind their own business. Or, alternatively—perhaps a different text—that it was all part of the game?

Well, supposing you take it over—even though you may not be a Buddha?

Not be a Buddha! What next! What else could any sentient being be?

Very well, then, why does manifestation occur?

'Seem to' occur. Why does a kitten seem to chase her own tail?

I doubt if she knows. Do you?

Does it matter? It just i s—like a hydrogen bomb on a big city.

Then h o w does manifestation occur?

I have told you, via three spatial dimensions, and one temporal. That renders it perceptible.

How does the temporal dimension operate?

By ksāna—*split seconds.*

How long do they last?

They represent the lower limit of the measurement of time. Neither man nor machine has ever recorded one—as far as my superficial knowledge of the matter extends.

They are purely theoretical, therefore? And the higher limit of the measurement of time?

The speed of light.

But that speed is well-known!

Yes, but no speed beyond it: it represents a maximum, as ksāna *represent a minimum.*

A maximum of what?

Must they not necessarily be measurements of the speed of time itself? If they were not so, something could go faster. Moreover light travels at the same speed regardless of whether the observer is travelling towards the source of light or away from it.

What has that got to do with it?

If the speed of light were not a maximum it would seem to be travelling still faster when measured by an observer travelling towards its source.

Unless it were travelling in a further direction of measurement, which should render all movements in lesser dimensions equidistant from itself.

Because they are at right-angles to it? That is so, at least so it appears to me, and it attributes to light the dimension which belongs to time itself.[1]

Which should make nonsense of 'light-years' as a measurement of distance?

Apparently, but are we metaphysicians pretending to be physicists, or physicists pretending to be metaphysicians?

No pretentions to either. But, has time a velocity?

Is it possible that you are regarding time as something that i s? These are concepts, limited by the phenomenal apparatus that evolves them.

So that the concept of time attributes to itself the concept of velocity?

On old clocks that is referred to in the words Tempus Fugit.

A *tempus* that *fugits* is serial. Is the notion of sequence acceptable?

Without seeking to rival your Augustan Latin—No.

Seriality is the very quintessence of 'time'?

So it appears.

But are we ourselves anything but 'time'?

Because we must be regarding the three sensorially perceptible directions of measurement from a fourth—which happens to be that of 'time' as the duration of spatiality?

Quite so.

All right, but we have a spatial interest also, and so we had better call ourselves 'space-time', in full?

As good a name for us as any of these scientific tickets in bog-Latin!

[1] That light does in fact derive from this further dimension is more fully established in Ch. 90 and note, in reference to the concept of *quanta*. It is understood as manifesting that further dimension from which the observer as such must be perceiving. Therein it is not different from what 'he' is.

Since we evidently are everything that appears, or that is extended in the space-time context, the dimension from which we perceive a tridimensional universe must be that further direction of measurement; so the name is surely apposite.

And helpful. Nevertheless that does not tell us what is manifesting.

It cannot be told.

Why?

Why? The answer should be obvious. Because what is manifesting is what we are, which can only be referred to by the one pronoun—'I'.

We cannot objectify what we are?

Not as 'what is objectifying'—only as what is objectified.

Because we cannot see ourselves, as an eye cannot?

It is the old story: the sought is what is seeking for the sought, the seeker is the sought for which he is seeking.

The kitten trying to catch her own tail!

52. *Liberation from Self*

'SELF' AS an entity is merely an erroneous concept.

'Self' as a phenomenon, is like all phenomena, an appearance, devoid of autonomous nature.

In neither sense could there be a 'self'.

As such, an 'I' is totally absent in pure appearance; as an object, 'I' am not at all.

Completely to be penetrated by that understanding is liberation from bondage, nor could there be liberation without that total annihilation of the notion of phenomenal identity.

Is this so difficult? Is there anyone so densely conditioned that he is unable to see that an objective 'me' as such could not possibly be freed? No 'me' can be freed, because there is no 'me' at all; 'me's' are pink elephants. He might see the whole universe as void, but as long as he 'himself' is seeing it, 'himself' seeing, he is no nearer freedom, since freedom is very precisely freedom from his idea of 'himself'. His notion of his 'self' is his only bondage.

Note: That is why 'self-cultivation', in the wrong sense of a 'self' working to cultivate its 'self', is steadily affirming the obstacle it is seeking to remove. That also is why no 'self' has ever been 'enlightened', or ever will be. The contention that 'X' is enlightened is not so much a contradiction in terms as like maintaining that a bird in an empty cage is not captive.

53. Meditation (Analytical)

NEITHER MEDITATION, premeditation, or unpremeditation, will ever rid you of yourself, for it must necessarily always be 'you' who are meditating, premeditating, or unpremeditating to an end which seeks to abolish this notion of you who are doing it; and nothing meditated, premeditated, or unpremeditated, by you can ever do that. They may produce a result, or results, but never that one, which is the only one that matters.

Once more, the abolition of the notion of a 'self' which you already know is not what you are, and necessarily being what is required, neither sitting thinking, which is the only meaning of the action termed 'meditating', nor sitting thinking of not-thinking, which is a definition of the action termed 'premeditating', nor sitting not-thinking about not-thinking, which is a definition of 'unpremeditated' acting, can be a possible way to arrive at the dis-appearance of the conceptual appearance which impedes your apprehension of what you are.

◇   ◇   ◇

The understanding, or rational explanation, of seeing into our 'nature' is via phenomenal comprehension and noumenal apprehension, i.e.

Phenomenally comprehended:

> What (phenomenally) is, noumenally is not, and
> What is (noumenally), phenomenally is not.

Noumenally apprehended:

> What (phenomenally) is not, noumenally is, and
> What is not (noumenally), phenomenally is.

Note: As in the case of all pairs of opposites, phenomenally regarded noumenon and phenomenon in mutual negation are seen as void, but seen noumenally are ultimate potentiality.

54. *Ethics and All That*

IT IS *primaire* to separate 'love' and 'hate', to think of them apart, for the more powerful the one may be the more powerful the other must be also, since they are not two.

People unused to abstract thought are apt to assume the contrary, i.e. that the stronger the 'love' the weaker the 'hate', and *vice versa*, but whatever the superficial appearance, dual expressions of affectivity must necessarily have the potentiality of the affectivity which they are expressing, regardless of which aspect is apparent.

One aspect may appear more frequently than another, but each must have their mutual potential, and their potential is all that they can be said to be.

If you care to substitute 'good' and 'bad' for 'love' and 'hate', or any other of our pairs of conceptual judgements, emotive or intellectual, what is said above will be equally applicable, and will be true or false as you may find it. And well worth the consequent consideration. For each concept is valid only in function of its opposite.

55. Enlightenment

But how does anyone know when he is enlightened?
No one can answer that question except from his own experience.

Well, yours then?
One day I was asking myself why, when I seemed to see so much so clearly, I was not enlightened.

Naturally, and so?
So? So I sat down and let mind 'fast' —with that question latent.

And what happened?
As clear as a bell, and as loud as a trumpet, I heard the words: 'But, you dam'fool, you ARE'.

'Dam'fool'?
Yes, 'dam'fool' and all.

And then?
When I pulled out of it I noticed that so it was!

And how did you know it even then?
Oh, quite traditionally. As the Masters put it, 'I drank a glass of water and knew whether it was hot or cold'.

You are pulling my leg!
Perhaps t h e y were? It was a way they had! But an essential part of their message.

Will you please be serious for a change?
Sorry, old man, not in my tradition.

But I want to know about 'enlightenment'?
So do I.

But you know more.
Unlikely.

Come now, what is it?
It isn't!

Then what is it supposed to be?
What we are eternally.

You and I?
No, not you.

Not me?
No, only I.

Oh, that!
No, this, just THIS.

Here and now.
Quite so—HERE and NOW.

Thanks, old man. You are sure?
Quite, take a glass of water and see for yourself.

Won't a glass of wine do instead?
Surely, but make sure it is bien chambré!

Note: I must apologise for this chap, his levity is lamentable! All he means is that what he appears to be can never be anything else but whatever he appears to be, and that whatever-he-is can never be anything but 'enlightened'—whatever that may be.   *W.W.W.*

56. One May Doubt . . .

ONE MAY doubt whether it is nostalgia for our personal youth that moves us so deeply, via music or any other retrospective and almost reminiscent experience, rather than the residual of a previous 'incarnation' which is thus stirred into mnemonic activity.

But what could there be to reincarnate? What indeed, but need there be any 'thing'? This passion for 'things', this obsession with objects! Damn it all—there aren't any, and there never were! Why can't we understand that? 'Things' don't reincarnate.

Why not? Because there never were any, of course! Let us wake up once and for all to the nonsense of all that!

Lived before? When have we ever ceased to live? Where have we ever not lived? Let us wake up to what we are—then we may understand why we experience nostalgia for what we have been, for what we have known, and for a time when we lived so much more profoundly.

Note: There is no more a 'question' of 'reincarnation' than there is a 'question' of 'free-will and determination', and for the same reason: the entity concerned is mythological.

Note: 2. 'There never was a time when I did not exist, nor you, nor any of these kings. Nor is there any future in which we shall cease to be.' (*Bhagavad Gita* II, 12).

57. *Let Us Be Precise*

AN EXPRESSION such as 'the Self is nothing' is occasionally encountered, but whether this is intended as a statement of metaphysical truth, or is just careless misuse of language, it seems to demand analysis.

How could 'the Self' be 'nothing'?

If there were, or could be, such a thing as 'a Self' it would then and thereby be some thing.

Is not 'a Self' a contradiction in terms anyhow?

'Self', being necessarily subject, 'a' subject (or 'the' subject) is, also necessarily, an object, and so some 'thing'.

But, as we know, self neither is nor is not: all that the word can represent is the absence of both concepts.

Probably this expression is just an example of conditioned inability to in-see, to do otherwise than seek to objectify, to make an object of what is subjective—the unceasing making of objects whether awake or asleep. But to what could the making of objects lead other than to the making of bigger and better bombs? Which is not metaphysical truth.

Note: As long as we think of ourselves as 'a self' (capital or lower-case) are we not just 'you' and not I?

58. *Observations Concerning Rebirth*

IF ANYBODY maintains that the notion called 'rebirth' is not, semantically, nonsense, he has probably omitted to consider the meaning of the word. A body can be said to be 'born' and it can be said to 'die', for that says what the words mean. The body dies, decays, dissolves, and disappears forever—that is 'death'. Only a 'thing', an object can 'die', and what other 'object' is there to suffer death? Only a body can be 'born', and what other object is there to suffer 'birth'? That which has died cannot be reborn, because death connotes dissolution. That which is born could not have *died*, without having been dissolved, which is an irreversible process of decay. The term 're-birth' at least makes good nonsense! No objective 'thing' could be *re*-born. It is unlikely that any true prophet has ever said it, and if they all had they could not have meant it, for it could not be true.

So what?

If no objective 'thing' could possibly be *re*-born, is it not equally certain and evident that whatever is non-objective could not possibly 'die', since there is no objective 'thing' to die, and the word itself is therefore not even applicable?

As long as anyone conceptualises an 'animus' of any kind whatever, he is like a child blowing bubbles, for he is necessarily inventing some objective 'thing' in his imagination, which could not exist as an *object*, and he does this because he is conditioned to objectify everything and because he correctly equates 'existing' with 'object'. But the subjective *does not 'exist' objectively at all*, and there is no form of existence that is other than objective, nor could there be—for to exist means that some 'thing' subsists in the seriality of time. And if that were understood, perhaps so much else would be understood that little pseudo-mystery would remain?

But the subjective (more accurately termed the non-objective, since it can have no definite characteristic, which would make it an object) cannot die, since there is no 'thing' to dissolve, and it cannot therefore be *re*born, nor, for the same reason, can it ever have been born at all. Being non-objective it is altogether outside the range of both birth and death, which are phenomenal events subject to Time. Nor can anything that is not an object be subject to time, nor anything objective be intemporal.

The non-objective, therefore, suffers neither birth nor re-birth, neither death nor re-death (each repetitive event as ludicrous as the other). And we can know nothing whatever that is other than a concept in mind, divided into what each sense may report, interpreted by cognition, such cognition being artificially divided into the somatic (physically experienced) and the psychic (imagined), all of which are necessarily objective and, by definition, interpretations of objectivisation.

Any conceptualisation whatever of the non-objective can only be metaphorical, not even hypothetical; it is figurative, a poetical image—since conceptualisation is visualising, and there is no 'thing' to visualise. And, *taken at all literally*, that which is metaphorical is nonsense.

You are objecting that what is meant is an association of an *animus* with two or more consecutive bodies that suffer birth and death in the apparent sequence of Time, and that the *animus*—if it is ever conceived as suffering birth—at least is never subject to death, if occasionally to damnation?

No doubt, but an *animus* as such, i.e. as an *object*, is only a concept, and it cannot be anything else, and concepts are the playthings of poets as of priests (and others) and are entirely vicarious when not pure images in mind. That is to say that concepts as such can have nothing but a conceptual existence.

The notion of subjectivity, cognisable only as 'I', and somewhat comically held responsible for almost everything that we do, cannot be born or reborn as has been explained, i.e. since 'I' lack any objective quality whatever, from which it might be assumed that subjectivity must always be hanging about ready to accept provisional association with any phenomenal manifestation that offered a vacancy. But the further one follows this romance the more ridiculous it becomes, if for no other reason than that it requires the entification of subjectivity and then the re-entification of what by definition, being non-objectivity, could have no 'ens'. Moreover all this performance is inevitably subject to duration—at least that part of it which we can imagine.

Well, such are the facts and conditions in so far as I can set them forth plausibly; let us make what we can of it. The Masters forbore to tell us. I wonder why?

59. *Vanity*

WHAT IS the most comical spectacle in the world?
Man.

Why? Or when?
Why, because of when.

By which you mean . . . ?
When he regards himself as, and takes it for granted that he is, the lord of the Earth and that the Universe was created expressly for himself so that he might exploit it according to his own good pleasure.

Is the former not a simple fact?
It is a simple appearance.

Is the latter not justified by the fact that he is able to do it?
That also is a simple appearance.

Since all is appearance anyhow, why is it comic?
Because in fact man is nothing.

Just a ghost?
Heavens, no! Not a ghost: nothing at all. No 'thing', just appearance.

A child building castles in sand?
No, there is no child: snow-man building snow-castles, if you wish.

Man is just a reflection?
Not even that.

Why?
A reflection is an accurate representation of some object. Man is not an accurate representation of anything.

What, then, is he?

A partial and distorted misrepresentation, composed of directions of measurement, of the absolute non-entity which is all that he is.

And so nothing to be conceited about!

No 'thing' to be any 'thing'.

Just a puppet?

With the risk of pandering to our vanity, and a little exaggeration, we may perhaps give our moustaches a twirl and pose as that!

60. *Bewildering Bits and Painful Pieces. III*

THE ESSENTIAL metaphysical principle is that every-thing cognisable is whatever we ourselves are and never anything that has any independent nature of its own.

⟡   ⟡   ⟡

'The world has been trying to solve its problem with a mind which is itself the problem.' What says that? The self-same mind!

Emptying the bath-water is useless unless the baby is emptied with it.

⟡   ⟡   ⟡

Mind is what I am, not something I own.
I have only to be what I am.

⟡   ⟡   ⟡

'He is enlightened' or 'he is not enlightened': what difference could there be? In either case he is still there.

Emptiness is *not being there* to be empty!

⟡   ⟡   ⟡

In a metaphysical statement there is always something that appears to be false, and something that appears to be true, so that the statement itself can be seen either as true or false; whereas in fact it is never either true or false but is always neither the one nor the other.

⟡   ⟡   ⟡

The answer to 'Who am I?'
Is, perhaps,
'Whoever is asking.'
For
I am
What I am
When I am not.

⟡   ⟡   ⟡

All I am is noumenon or Tao or Godhead. I must know it, but I lose it if I say it, for, in saying it, I am it no longer—since I have cast it forth as an object.

Man and Nature

When man thinks he is conquering Nature by exploiting Her, he is a figure of fun. He is making a fool of himself, and anybody who has eyes to see can see it, and laughs.

❖   ❖   ❖

Samsara, all phenomenality, is—the soughing of the wind.

❖   ❖   ❖

'There is no purpose: there is only a living beyond measure.' *(Krishnamurti)*.

❖   ❖   ❖

The shadow will disappear the moment its substance is no longer seen as such.

That is what constitutes the Supreme Vehicle as represented by T'ang Dynasty Ch'an.

❖   ❖   ❖

Suffering? Why are you suffering? Because you are a case of mistaken identity.

❖   ❖   ❖

'Dependent Origination' is the do-er: it constitutes the only bondage there could be. There is nobody to be bound: dependent origination cannot be bound; its dependent effects are bondage.

❖   ❖   ❖

If the sought is the seeker, then the seeker must be the sought, and the seeking must be the finding, and the finding the seeking.

PART IV

TIME

As long as one accepts 'time' tacitly as such
he is dreaming a dream, not living a life.

61. Definitions

'*Passing-time*' implies sequential duration.

'*Time*' is a generic name for all forms of temporality including the measurement of motion in space.

Duration designates the essential aspect of all categories of temporality, mutable and immutable.

Intemporality and *eternity* seek to imply total absence of a time concept, as well as the concept of infinite or circular duration.

This terminology reveals *(a)* the vagueness with which temporal concepts are surrounded and *(b)* the fact that we are not capable of conceiving the total absence of time. This latter applies also to space, for 'infinity' implies unending continuity of space in a time context, as 'intemporality' and 'eternity' imply an unending continuity of time in a space context. It will appear that time is an interpretation of a measurement of space that is not within the limitations of sensory perception, so that the physical concept of space-time is justifiable also metaphysically.

62. *The Low-down on Time*

PHENOMENALLY, the 'present' is merely theoretical, for the complicated chemico-physiological process, which every kind of sensorial perception involves, requires an apparent passage of time.

Therefore events and objects of which we are cognisant are already in what we call the 'past' when we become aware of them, or *they should be if they factually occurred as events external to the mind that cognises them.* So that, in fact, there is no such state as the 'present', since what it purports to manifest is no longer in manifestation, *unless the apparent occurrence of events is in fact the cognising of them.*

The 'past' is a mnemonic depository, maintained by means of engrams; it is inconstant, developing incessantly and deteriorating progressively, and has only a psychological existence, which is the existence of a dream-structure. Therefore phenomenally there is neither factual 'present' nor factual 'past'.

The 'future' is only imagined, and is constructed mentally under the influence of hope and fear, unless, of course, *it exists eternally unextended in space-time.* It cannot be considered as having any phenomenal existence whatever, so that phenomenally neither past, present nor future exist at all except as conceptual suppositions.

Noumenally, 'past' and 'future', being phenomenal concepts, can have no independent existence; noumenally there can only be an eternal (intemporal, timeless) 'present' which, phenomenally, is neither present nor absent.

And this is what is inferred in the passages italicised above.

63. 'I am This, Here, Now!'

Why Awakening is not a Personal Experience

UNDERSTANDING IS 'sudden' (a flash), i.e. im- or non-mediate, because it is intemporal. It is understanding of intemporality, and, therefore, it can only be 'sudden', that is time-less.

It is then necessarily understanding from the superior dimension which comprehends those we know and which are subject to Time.

This understanding is so 'sudden' that our psyche is incapable of registering it. That is why it is not a phenomenal, a psycho-somatic 'experience'—although a phenomenon may be the medium whereby it occurs.

Note: This higher direction of measurement is not 'beyond' those we use normally: those which we know are elements of it, as length and breadth are elements of volume; 'ours' are within it, parts of it, technically. That is why the flash of fuller vision is released by a sensory percept, and why there is no 'beyond' to seek for—since it is always 'here'. In fact it is very precisely 'where' we are; and what we are is evident as soon as we perceive fully at last! It is our centre.

64. *Analysis of Intemporality*

I

WE ALL perceive volume, for every event is extended
in the three directions of measurement by which volume is
constituted, and which we call length, breadth and height
(or depth). But if we who are perceiving were within that
volume we could not perceive it as such, i.e. as an object.
We can perceive our 'own' hands and feet as being within it,
and any parts of 'our' bodies that are objects to what is
perceiving, but we cannot perceive what is actually perceiving. It must necessarily follow from this fact that what is
perceiving does not lie in any of the objective directions of
measurement that constitute volume or space. Expressed
otherwise, since the 'perceiver' is the subject of the object
perceived, i.e. volume, 'he' can never perceive 'himself' as
the perceiving subject.

Where, then, is what is perceiving? There must be a
centre from which *perceiving* as a faculty, operates, from
which it is functioning subjectively, and since that centre
cannot lie within the three objective dimensions it must be
'beyond' them. But 'beyond' does not imply a spatial situation
such as 'above' or 'below', it merely asserts that the position
is inaccessible objectively. Therefore that position must be
in a direction of measurement other than the three that we
know. It must also be at right-angles to each of the other
three, as each of the three is to each other, and it must
include volume as volume includes all three (length, breadth,
height).

This, then, it is which is perceiving every single
thing that 'we' think 'we' perceive, and the inevitable
'centre' from which all directions of measurement must
necessarily be measured must, with equal inevitability
necessarily be—where? Where else in the cosmos could it be,
but *here*? Always, and in all circumstances, it must be HERE.
Here, then is where what is perceiving must be, here is where
whatever we ourselves are must be, and here is the centre
of the superior dimension whose superior 'volume' includes
that with which we are objectively familiar. A lot of verbiage

in order to demonstrate what can be seen in a single flash of intuition, but demonstration can be a comforting confirmation.

Such, clearly, is the subjective centre on behalf of which each of us says 'I', and equally clearly, the objective centre with which each of us is identified is that tri-dimensional object whose volume bears whatever name we each have been given by baptism or otherwise, only certain exterior portions of which are perceptible to us when subjected to observation. The two should now be quite distinct: the subjective centre situated in a superior and all-inclusive dimension, common to all perceiving of tri-dimensional objects, and vicarious *interpretation* via such tri-dimensional objects within their psychic framework limited by the three dimensions of space, which interpetation is what we know as 'form'.

This extra-dimensional centre is what subjectively we are as 'I', and *that*, tri-dimensionally revealed, is what objectively we each *appear to be* as 'me'. Since it is we who perceive and since we perceive one another interpretated tri-dimensionally as form, it cannot be otherwise. Spatially regarded, that seems evident and clear, but what is it that enables us to perceive and to be perceived—for we must 'last' in order to *be perceived*, that is to say that form must be extended objectively not only in space but also in duration. What then is it that lasts, that has apparent duration and sequence in time? We can know of nothing but form itself, which is clearly only objectivisation of what is objectifying its own subjectivity.

It surely follows that the duration of objectified form can only be an aspect of what form itself is, perceived serially or in sequence? That mode of perceiving form must necessarily be a dimension of the perceiving of form, another direction of measurement or 'angle' on form, rendered perceptible tri-dimensionally in that manner called serial or sequential. If volume were perceived directly, should it not appear in four dimensions, should it not be complete? But it is clearly not complete, form is incomplete in itself since it requires sequence, since it cannot appear at all without duration. Time, therefore, is a necessary element of form, and that element can only be a dimension whose direction as such is not perceptible to our sensorial apparatus subject to tri-dimensional limitation.

Is it not evident that transcendent volume can only reveal objects, can only fulfil the requirements of manifestation, i.e. of the objectification of what we are, by employing what we know as seriality or sequential duration, by revealing them in a temporal context which is itself an interpretation of one of its own directions of measurement?

II

'SPACE-TIME' IS, therefore, an accurate term for the mechanism whereby objectification becomes perceptible in three directions of measurement, or volume.

But what in fact is operating this process of phenomenal manifestation which constitutes our world, our life, our dream? The answer seems obvious: we are operating it: there is rigorously no one else available to do it! And if it seemed possible to imagine anyone else, it would soon be apparent that such 'other', deity or not, was in fact none other than what we 'ourselves' ultimately must be.

To look for an entity would be absurd, nor is it an entity that we find when we look. What we find or infer is the centre from which each direction of measurement diverges, the eye at the measuring-end of each right-angled measuring-rod, an eye which however is not a noun spelled e-y-e-, but a pronoun spelled 'I', that is to say not any object, but the subject of every dimension so measured. This 'I', however, is measuring itself, for the measuring is the mechanism of objectification, since only in the resulting volume can phenomena become apparent.

The measuring in fact is not directly performed by a measurer: the measuring is an interpretation of the process, devised via the psyche of the objectivised, and is recorded subject to that phenomenon's dimensional limitations in his dualised dialectic. The dimensions thus imagined are, then, simply what the thus objectified measurer is, they are 'his' dimensions, measurements of 'himself', and they are all, absolutely all that we can ever know of 'him' personally regarded as an object, i.e. objectified figuratively in mind.

There is no 'he': 'he' is I, always, everywhere I, and never anything but I, objectively everything phenomenally cognisable, subjectively no thing whatever, absolutely no thing, but just I, and always here, always now, devoid of any kind of objective existence whatever—apart from the totality of the phenomenal dream which is our world. Such 'I', of course, is universal, and so is what we all are. That is why the measurements of the measurer are the measurer—and the measurer is what we are. Therefore the dimensions are ours, and the centre from which all directions of measurement diverge is our centre and a clear definition of all that we could ever be.

What we are must necessarily be what we can understand as the ultimate all-embracing and inter-penetrating dimension, three directions of measurement of which are all that our sensorial apparatus is developed to perceive.

This which we are, then, though *in-dividual*, i.e. undivided, is no sort of entity, since no objective quality whatever can be attributed to 'it', and that which, objectified as phenomenon, 'it' becomes in manifested appearance though *dividual*, i.e. divided, has no sort of *ens* either, since all that is not merely apparent, i.e. form, is the non-entity which is thus manifesting as form and appearance. Metaphysically, of course, 'it' is neither dividual nor individual, but the total conceptual absence of both.

III

FORM IS dependent on duration: without duration there is no form. The concept of form is consequent to the concept of sequence itself. Intemporally form is formless. That is why 'form is void, and void is form', as stated in the Heart Sutra.

Form, therefore, is a phenomenon due to perception from a direction of measurement 'beyond' or 'within' those available to a psychic apparatus, such further direction being cognised as duration. That is why form is found to be 'illusory' when a further direction of measurement becomes accessible to a psyche. Form suddenly ceases to be real (a 'thing') at the moment of such 'awakening', since the dimension interpreted hitherto as duration has been revealed as a volume in which tri-dimensionality is henceforth included.[1]

This all-inclusive volume, *transcendent and inherent*, is known as 'intemporality', perfectly so called since its manifestation is known as 'time', whereby the temporal character of this volume is recognised as a measurement and interpreted as the fourth dimension of form. It can now be comprehended that form is not a structure as such *within* a dimensional *framework*, as may have been supposed, but is in fact an appearance *whose composition consists entirely of directions of measurement* perceived from the source thereof.

Intemporality or the voidness of form, comprising four directions of measurement, in three of which form is manifested with the fourth interpreted as duration, is to be regarded as the superior and all-inclusive volume from which tri-dimensional volume is observed, as only plane-surfaces and straight lines should be observable from the third. Therefore it is precisely because this extra-dimensional volume from which we observe represents what we are as 'I', that we cannot know it objectively and so have to express it as 'time' in order that form may be cognisable—since, without that duration and seriality, form in three-dimensional volume could not be perceived.

It follows that time, as a measurement of space, as one of the four directions of measurement that compose fourfold super-volume, is an element of our appearance, and that 'Space-time'—volume and duration which manifest form—is simply a technical definition of whatever we are in the process of objectivisation.

Apart from what we are as objectified appearance we are, by definition, no things; we *are not* as anything whatever —for we would need to be something in order to be cognisable, and as there can be no subjective 'thing' to be cognised,

---

[1] Which is why 'awakened' Masters, although 'awake' can still perceive tri-dimensionally as theretofore.

so there cannot be any cogniser that could either cognise or be cognised as an object—since what is implied is the subject of all cognition. A conceptual subject of cogniser, cognising, and cognition could not be cognisable, for a cognising seeker is the cogniser sought, and the cogniser sought is the cognising seeker.

Therefore what we are is intemporal, just as what we appear to be is temporal, and intemporality is what constitutes the Nth. dimension, which, as 'N', also represents Noumenon.

Note: In case confusion should arise regarding the meaning of the terms 'direction of measurement' and 'dimension', they both connote *measurement*, but the former more specifically indicates a direction at right-angles to all other directions (only three of which are sensorially cognisable); the latter, when the sense requires it, can also imply 'volume'—the volume resulting from such right-angled measurements as may be specified. For example, 'volume' comprises three or more 'directions of measurement', each of which is also known as a 'dimension', as is the resulting 'volume' itself.

65. Definition of Noumenon

NOUMENON IS the subjective aspect of phenomenon, which is the objective aspect of it, the former negative, the latter positive.

Phenomena can have no apparent existence apart from noumenon whose objectivisation they are as appearance.

Noumenon has no existence, apparent or non-apparent, other than as a concept.

Therefore, having neither being nor non-being, 'Noumenon' represents the total absence of both as objects of cognition, whereby it remains as a verbal symbol representing the source and origin of conceptuality itself—which, of course, includes all possible cognition.

And it is inconceivable because conceptuality cannot conceive its source.

Note: It would seem, therefore, that the term 'noumenon' may be used either as the counterpart of 'phenomenon' or in order to indicate the non-objective source of all cognition, according to the context. The true counterpart of 'phenomenon' is just 'non-phenomenon', the mutual negation of which is the conceptual absence of non-phenomenon—which is Noumenon.

66. Discussing Intemporality

THOUGHT IS discursive, and therefore subject to the seriality of time. That is why thought is to be avoided in seeking to awaken to intemporality, and the only and sufficient reason for such avoidance.

The 'one thought' or 'thought of the Absolute' or 'Absolute thought', according to the fancy of the translator, spoken of by Shen Hui, is non-discursive, instantaneous, spontaneous and without cognisable duration. Whatever duration it acquires is acquired phenomenally, subject to space-time, interpreted as an *after*-thought, which is to say that the original *ap*prehension is rendered dualistically *com*prehensible. When that happens the 'one thought' has already been lost, and awakening has been by-passed.

Every 'event' that becomes dialectically comprehensible is subject to space-time. Noumenality is entirely intemporal, and only the intemporal is what-we-are as opposed to the temporal which is our appearance manifested *as* space-time. All sensorial experience is temporal; only when mind is 'fasting' are we in a state of availability. That is the explanation, simple and obvious, of the essential teaching of the Masters, as of the imagined and suggested 'methods' for rendering 'us' available for reintegration into conscious intemporality.

Conceptuality, therefore, is an absolute barrier to direct integration. This comprehension should abolish all the apparent doctrinal 'mysteries'. Religions try to teach this, but without understanding it; they make a holy mystery of it, and erect upon it an overwhelming structure of abstract and concrete mythology. A Way no doubt it may be, but one that is necessarily devious in the extreme.

II

ALL FORMS of 'discrimination' and 'meditation' imply activity of a dualistic or split mind, whose apparent operation is *dependent on duration*, or, if they do not imply that, then these terms are not being used to carry the only meaning which etymologically they can carry, and are therefore inadmissible in this context, for without semantic exactitude accurate understanding is no longer feasible. Similarly 'spiritual discipline', methods, techniques and practices, of whatever description, are all necessarily volitional and *subject to duration*, so that all such forms of endeavour are incompatible with reintegration into intemporality, and must be obstacles to its occurrence.

All this seems to have been familiar to the great Chinese metaphysical philosopher Chuang Tzu, the supreme exponent of Tao, as it was to his predecessor Lao Tzu. His teaching of non-volitional action and fasting of the mind, being intemporal indicates the way which surely leads directly to inseeing into intemporality, a teaching that was subsequently incorporated, somewhat obscured by mysticism, into Mahāyāna Buddhism, and reached its apogee in the Supreme Vehicle as preached by the great awakened Masters of the T'ang dynasty, a teaching which still survives, though in decline, in modern Ch'an and in Japanese Zen.

III

LIBERATION IS freedom from the bondage of duration —since the apparent 'bondage' of phenomenal identification is entirely an effect of seriality or 'time'. Also whatever may be implied by the notions of *karma* and 're-birth', they are all causal, dependent on sequence, are temporal phenomena, so that, as is taught, they must immediately disappear with integration into intemporality.

The apparent universe is manifested in mind, via the five senses which appear to perceive it and the sixth which cognises it, and it is *exclusively composed* of the three components, the directions of phenomenal measurement, or 'space', and the fourth measurement which is time, the whole constituting an objectivisation of the non-objective, and so formless and 'void' super-volume which is Intemporality.

Thus the phenomenal universe is Intemporality or Noumenon objectively manifest in tridimensional volume by means of the seriality of 'time'. Reintegrated, it is just intemporal noumenality.

IV

WE CANNOT conceive anything otherwise than in a time-context. Intemporality is rigorously unthinkable, that is impossible to conceive. This simple statement explains why 'thought' and 'conceptuality' are always held up to us by the Masters as the obstacle to 'awakening'.

Awakening is waking up from the dream of serial time into the normal state of what intemporally we are. Why are we not able to cognise intemporality conceptually? Why is intemporality inconceivable?

Do you not see the answer? Who is trying to cognise whom? What is chasing what? Tails not caught by their kittens!

Why cannot we objectify *Intemporality*?

There are not two minds. That is the reason. Great Masters as far apart in time and in space as Huang Po and Ramana Maharshi, both said it categorically, in a Buddhist and a Vedantist context respectively, and all the great Masters implied it.

A 'mind' as such cannot be supposed to *seek* to objectify that by which it is able to objectify, since, so doing, it would be objectifying what it itself is. Only volition *seeks*, and mind does not respond. How could an objectivising mind objectify the objectivising mind which is objectivising?

This which is objectivising from intemporality is here being called 'mind', but there are not two, nor are they different. How could there be two, how could they be different? Have we two phenomenal heads? Or even one? They are just two conceptual images, used for descriptive purposes, the one in psychological terminology, the other in that of physics, and both are provisional descriptions of what we are.

67. *Constitution of Phenomena*

ALL OBJECTS are composed of our three directions of measurement plus duration, by means of which they are perceptible as form.

Form is constituted by the measurements *which are also its perceiving*, and the perceiving is thereby demonstrated as identical with that which is perceived. Form being only its perceiving, there remains no room for a perceiver as such. Perceived form is itself perceiver, perceiving, and perceived. This, pointed out by Padma Sambhava and other Masters, and often reiterated by the unconvinced, dimensionally regarded seems to be evident and inevitable.

Nor is there any room for a 'projector' of form—in case there should be a lingering nostalgia for such a superfluous non-entity: the imagined 'projector' is the perceiver, and there is no 'thing' to be projected: here 'things' become apparent, they do not exist as 'things', and their perceiver is all that they are. The only 'event' is a perceiving of form, and the mechanism of such 'event' is measurement in three directions, called 'space' and a fourth called 'time', and such perceiving is the totality of the 'event'—its origin, its constitution, and its appearance: its perceiving is the perceived.

Have we not disposed of duality? Have we not exposed it as a theory that is not in accordance with the facts, as an inaccurate interpretation like the theory that the Earth is flat, or the thesis that the sun revolves round the Earth? Is it not just an error of judgement based on superficial appearance? All the conceptual entities habitually introduced into the picture are seen to be figments of the imagination, disordered at that, and quite superfluous. Fictions, all fictions! The supposed 'event' is just the perceiving of the supposed 'event', and its perceiving is its manifestation, which is its dimensional composition. There simply is no place in the picture either for 'subject' or for 'object'. All that can be found is the apparent or phenomenal 'event' itself, a sensorial perceiving which is an aspect of the noumenality which is all that it is. What we are is not separate from what we perceive, and what we perceive is not separate from what we are. Objects are not separate from subject, nor subject from objects, phenomena are not separate from noumenon, nor noumenon from phenomena. Nothing phenomenal is separate from what noumenally we are—and that is absolutely devoid of appearance. As concepts we are non-conceptuality, as figments composed of space-time we are in-finite in-temporality. What more is there to be said?

Note: Are we worrying about further attributes of form, that is to say quality and function? Materials, characteristics, whatever a 'form' appears to 'perform', whether it be machine or animal? These are interpretive concepts, dependent on 'time' and based on 'habit-energy' or memory. These apparent activities are psychic elaborations, details completing the phenomenal picture, for which nothing additional whatever is either required or produced. Affective and intellectual manifestations are also interpretive psychic elaborations of apparent complexity, but this does not imply that their phenomenal expression is ever directly noumenal. That is why the attempted attribution, by simple-minded and pious people, of such concepts and emotions to a divine, i.e. noumenal, origin, for example 'divine love', is quite inaccurate and deceptive. All this is clearly revealed in the few hundred words of the little Heart Sutra, if correctly spoken— read subjectively as by the Bodhisattva Avalokiteshvara speaking, not objectively as by a seeking pupil, though at first sight the form of its expression, as rendered by translators *desperately* trying to objectify everything, may appear to conceal it.

II

LET US analyse these psychic elaborations a little by following the pattern of the Heart Sutra.

Phenomena		*Skandha*	
'Form'	is the *perceiving*	of form,
'Thinking'	is the *conceiving*	of percepts,
'Acting'	is the *conating*	of concepts,
'Events'	are the *being conscious*	of conation.

Affectivity is inherent in volitional acting, as Intellection is inherent in thinking.

None of the *skandha* has other than a conceptual existence: they are an analytical apparatus that seeks to demonstrate that phenomenal life and the so-called 'Cosmos'

are the *being conscious* of living in an apparent Cosmos
subject to time and space which themselves represent what,
dimensionally regarded, we are.

Therefore there can be no question of their being
five separate 'things': they are not separated, nor are they
'one'. They, also, are a phenomenalised aspect of what we
are, which is I.

The five senses are concerned with perceiving, and
the sixth with cognising perception. The five *skandha* cover
the resulting total psychic mechanism, analytically, up to
and including consciousness of events. In general the *skandha*
represent both perceiving and the interpretation of perception.

Form or appearing is a functioning—*prajñāic*
functioning whose static aspect is *dhyanic*—whereby 'mind'
objectifies itself by means of subjective and objective
alternation. Basically there is only perceiving and cognising,
which are this *functioning* which is all that we can be said
to be.

> 'There is neither creation nor destruction,
> Neither destiny nor free-will,
> Neither path nor achievement:
> This is the final truth.'
>
> *Sri Ramana Maharshi*

68.   The Nature of the Cosmos

WE ARE the nature of the cosmos, and it has no other.
There is nothing religious about the cosmos,
Because there is nothing religious about what we are.

That is the fact of the matter. 'We', of course, are
all sentient beings,
And what we are is I.

The simple truth is that:
Temporality is not separate from Intemporality, and
vice versa.
Nothing temporal is separate from what intemporally
we are.
Which is totally devoid of appearance.
Difference is apparent (phenomenal) only.

Phenomenally all difference seems to be absolute:
that is the difference of all dualities; but non-dually, in total
conceptual absence, no such 'difference' can appear, for
difference itself is a concept.

In this total conceptual absence there is neither
object conceived nor subject conceiving: I-functioning am
no longer functioning as subject of object. I am no longer
split. Split, I am temporality; whole, I know no 'time'.

Conceptual negation cannot be conceived, nor can
it be 'one'—which is a concept: it is just not at all as anything
that can be conceived as any thing. Why? Because what it is,
is what I am who am not conceiving.

It is what we are, neither anything nor nothing. It is
just I—not even I-*ness*. We, as I, are this time-less in-finity.
But what timeless infinity? What infinite intemporality
could we be but 'I am (THIS) that I am'?

Comment

It is apt to take people a long time to see this. Perhaps
it is too obvious to be seen easily. But, once seen, should it
not be difficult indeed not to see it?

The phrase 'is too obvious' really implies that it is
here all the time, 'just in front of your eyes' as the Masters

said it: like the spectacles through which you look without seeing *them*.

More accurately, since 'it' cannot be objectivised, a subjective displacement is needed in order to 'be' it, even intuitionally: perhaps the subjective displacement which, permanently effected, is awakening from the nightmare of 'bondage'.

69.   T.N.T.

Would you be offended if I told you that someone had said
that you were a fool?

How could that be possible? Only an object can suffer offence.

No doubt, and perhaps only a fool at that! But what of it?

Damn it, I am not an object!

So you cannot be offended?

*I cannot possibly be offended. Nor can I be the object of the
supposedly offensive epithet either.*

Why is that?

For the same reason: only an object can be a fool.

So that in fact you cannot be a fool either?

*As what I am, that is to say as 'I', I cannot be an object of any
kind whatever. Very simple indeed!*

Also, perhaps, revealing!

Does it not lead straight in?

But there are fools! Who, then, are they? Who is a fool, or
whatever it may be, anything whatever if you prefer, when
so-called, so-judged, so-categorised?

*Whoever so-calls, so-judges, so-categorises, of course! Who else
could they be? Who else is, or could conceivably be, concerned?*

Not the object, but the subject?

*The object in question is only the s u b j e c t ' s object. The
inferred object, to whom the epithet is applied, is untouched and
untouchable. The idea, the judgement, epithet, or whatever it is
and however inspired, is entirely confined to the mind that
conceives it, and it exists nowhere else in any form whatever
except as a rumour.*

It belongs to its own subject?

*Quite so: its own subject has thereby assumed objective identi-
fication with a phenomenal concept.*

But does that not apply to every personal observation?

Yes, and it applies to every utilisation of the pronoun 'you'.

It seems to me that every objective judgement must thereby be rendered inapplicable!

Not at all! Its application is thereby restored to where it belongs, which is to the conceiving subject instead of to an object to which it was being adventitiously applied.

Why adventitious?

Because that object as such could have no independent existence and is therefore incapable of possessing any attribute or characteristic.

Which can only mean that no object can ever have an independent existence or possess any attribute or characteristic!

Of course! Of course! Can you not see that so it must necessarily be?

But this is more destructive than any hydrogen bomb that has ever been conceived, even by a writer of science-fiction!

Are bombs based on nuclear fission anything but phenomenal toys, noise and pother appearing to destroy what has never existed?

Including some five hundred thousand human-beings. . . .

Also some million beetles, and some ten million sentient-beings (various). Necessarily a mixed bag of mutual appearances. You surely are not regarding them as possessing any kind of existence?

Evidently not as regards what appears to be 'destroyed', but this 'bomb' of *yours* seems to wipe out all knowledge.

Objective knowledge, supposed knowledge of suppositional objects, must inevitably lie exposed as what it is—but that is not total destruction, though if it were we could not hesitate for a second to pull the switch, since it must be seen for what it is. The knowledge you speak of is of limited, of closely restricted application. It applies to the sphere to which it belongs, which is the relative sphere of phenomenal manifestation.

And what relation is there between the two spheres?

None. There is a solution of continuity, 'phenomenally regarded', between phenomenality and its noumenon.

Whyever should that be?

The reason is because, 'noumenally regarded', they are not separate, and where there is no separation there cannot be a continuity to be dissolved.

So that what *is* noumenally, phenomenally *is not*? And what phenomenally *appears to be*, noumenally *is not*?

Thus must it be as long as Intemporality manifests as Time.

70. *Father Time*

I

CONSCIOUSNESS CONCEPTUALISED is conventionally designated by a variety of pairs of interdependent counterparts: for instance 'Heaven (the Kingdom of)' and 'Earth', 'Nirvana' and 'Samsara', 'Noumenon' and 'Phenomena', the two former religious and ancient, the latter modern and philosophical. Metaphysically we may add a fourth: 'Intemporality' and that which is 'Temporal' or subject to time.

What we are, on the basis of consciousness and sentience, is intemporal, and what we appear to be—our objective appearance with which, alas, we are conditioned to become identified—is temporal. That is equivalent to stating that what subjectively 'we' represent is 'timeless', and that what we think we are is 'time'.

'*Is* time'? Yes, for what we think we are is something in action, is *doing*, is whatever we *do*, physically or psychically as psycho-somatic apparatus. That is *karma*, apparently volitional acting and the corresponding apparently volitional reaction to that. Each such apparent action is an 'event', and our phenomenal world is a composite structure of 'events' extended in time—for each must have apparent duration in order to extend in apparent space and so manifest perceptually.

This movement, however, does not make us entities acting *in* 'time', or subject to 'time': it leaves us as all that 'time' is; we neither pass through some thing, foreign to what we are, called 'time', nor does some thing called 'time' pass through us. There is no such objective thing or object as 'time' or 'duration': the concept represents the apparent duration which renders possible the perceiving of the apparent movements or actions as a result of which we objectify ourselves as actors or doers, and on which depends our supposition that we exist as autonomous entities.

'Time' has no other existence, has no existence of its own, is not at all apart from sentient perceiving. Therefore all that 'Time' can be is a term for the serial aspect of what we think we are or appear to be as phenomena. And all that in fact we are is intemporality.

II

The Secondary Aspect of Time

'TIME', CONCEPTUALISED as an object, could never make sense, for it has no objective existence whatever. It is just our sequential living. It is, perhaps, the living itself of life. We objectify it by means of clocks, and persuade ourselves that clocks measure 'it', whereas what they are measuring is our life. When we miss or catch a train we miss or catch a clock. When we measure the duration of day and night, childhood and age, we are measuring our own seriality and calling it 'time'. *Tempus* does not *fugit:* it is our sequential living which is seen as fleeting. 'Time' is an invention, a hypothesis developed by our urge to objectivise the subjective: the word represents an aspect of our volition to affirm ourselves as entities functioning in a universe of objects of which we are the autonomous subjects. We have invented it as an element of self-affirmation. There is no such 'thing', never was, never could be. It is an objectivisation of the sequential aspect of ourselves. It is simply our apparent duration which we have tried to separate from ourselves and have turned into a 'thing' in its own right. We have set it up as if it were something independent, made an image of it (Father Time), put it on a pedestal, sometimes worshipping it as a golden calf, sometimes regarding it as an enemy and using it as a coconut-shy! Not in any circumstance of our living seriality is it ever any thing but that apparent seriality itself.

❖   ❖   ❖

It follows, therefore, that the primary aspect of time, or duration, by means of which all phenomena become perceptible is an element inherent in our own subjectivity, and whatever we attribute to 'time' is part and parcel of our perceiving. Necessarily, then, it must be a dimension of what we are, indeed must it not be a direction of measurement which is other than the three which produce the appearance of form (length, breadth and height), which is volume? What indeed can it be but a further direction of measurement interpreted, not spatially like the other three, but rendered perceptible only as sequence or duration, that is an integral element in our phenomenalisation whereby we become apparent as objects—as objects which appear to last?

But such directions of measurement, spatial or interpreted as sequence, are not objects as such. They are, so to speak, measurements of what we are from the centre of what we are, a 'centre' which being of infinity is ubiquitous. They represent conceptually what we are, measuring itself in order to manifest itself, noumenon becoming phenomenal by means of tri-dimensional volume and duration. They are conceptualised in order that what intemporally we are may be analysed and understood, but they have no objective existence as things-in-themselves. They are no more than a schema whereby we may comprehend, as far as that may be possible, *this* our intemporality in the process of becoming manifest as *that* temporal phenomenon.

❖   ❖   ❖

Let me repeat, perfect understanding cannot result from the visualising of objects, and that because the subject of objects is itself an object. Such comprehension is temporal, which is derivative, limited, and there is a *solution of continuity* between the comprehension of mind which is divided into subject and object, and the apprehension of mind which is whole. There is no 'mind', either, as an objective entity, there is only Intemporality, which is no 'thing' at all, and such is all that we are.

To attempt to define Intemporality would be *de facto* absurd—for temporality would then be trying to define what it is not, and subject cannot be defined by its object, for subject would then be defining itself and thereby making itself an object which is precisely what it could never be.

When 'I', searched for, disappears, Maharshi said, there appears 'I-I' by itself, and this is the Infinite. It is also the Intemporal. To attempt to say anything as simply and clearly as Maharshi said it may also be absurd, but—as he surely knew—it must be said again and again and in such other ways as may be attempted.

'Time' as duration is an element of what we appear to be, like length and breadth, together called 'plane-surface', with height constituting 'volume', but as such it is an interpretation of the noumenality which is what we are. Its appearance is temporality, but its sub-stance is intemporal, just as the appearance of volume (or form) is finite, the sub-stance of which is infinite.

Therefore what we call space-time manifests as phenomenality, but unmanifested is noumenon. And intemporality, infinity, and noumenality are concepts whose only, inconceivable, expression is 'I'.

Note: It may be well to remember that we are conditioned normally to think *as* from a supposedly autonomous entity turning every percept and intuition into a conceptualised object.

This is the famous 'guest' position instead of the 'Host', the 'minister' instead of the 'Prince', the 'functional' position instead of the 'Principal'. So-thinking we can only turn round in circles, chasing our own tails, never can we escape from our 'selves'. So-reading the Sutras and the words of the great Masters never shall we understand, never *could* we understand—for such must be the cognition of split-mind.

When obdurate translators so render the words of the Masters, as, alas, is all too frequently the case, their translations are—just plain *wrong*. The position of 'Host', 'Prince', or 'Principal' we have only to assume, for such we are, and unless we so think and speak and write and translate we are misleading those who listen to or read our words.

In so far as any statement explicitly or implicitly is congruent with the concept of objective space-time, in such degree it cannot be an expression of suchness or 'truth' which itself can only be in-finite and in-temporal.

71. 'Psychological Time'

PEOPLE OFTEN speak of 'psychological' time, but that is only a derivative of astronomical time, a personal notion, individual time. Whereas astronomical time represents the duration which is inherent in all phenomenal manifestation, 'psychological' or 'individual' or 'personal' time represents identification, i.e. the identified pseudo-entity thinking in a temporal context.

It should be evident that anyone so-thinking is thereby accepting the phenomenal world of appearance as 'real', and himself as an autonomous entity therein, calculating in terms of objective duration something that 'he' as an object is doing. Such an one is bound psychologically by 'psychological time', which is a concept of split-mind.

Astronomical time, on the contrary, can be accepted as inherent in manifestation since it is then the duration without which no manifestation could appear to occur. It is an element of temporality, and temporality is the phenomenal aspect of the intemporality which is what noumenally we are. An awakened Master may recognise it for what it is as appearance, whereas 'psychological time' is an element of bondage.

72. *What is Time?*

I

IN CONSIDERING the problem of 'time' it should be desirable to understand wnat people in general mean by the word. Let me take two examples from newspapers, one French and the other English, which happen to be in front of me. The French one refers to '*la marche objective et inexorable du temps*'. That statement appears to be a typical example of the view according to which we stand apart observing the passage of time, which appears to be objective and inexorable, i.e. a force foreign to ourselves and to events, to which we and events are all subjected. The English one states 'It (time) is not a rolling stream—for who is standing on the bank to see it? It is we who do the rolling, not time. And all this rolling has to be related to the chance revolutions of a solar system, for convenience . . . but for whose convenience?' This statement takes the opposite point of view: 'time' does not move at all, it is we who move through a stationary 'time', and it distinguishes between time as duration and time as a measurement of duration. Both are intelligent and, I think, reliable examples of current attitudes towards temporality. It will be observed, however, that in both 'time' is regarded objectively, as some force foreign to ourselves, through which we pass or which passes through us. In both 'we' are seen as phenomenal individuals.

Considering the matter more generally, we in the West regard 'time' as beginning in the past: we speak of 'past, present and future' and not 'future, present and past'. No doubt there lies at the back of our minds the concept that God created the world at some past moment of time and that it evolves towards an unknown future, and also that each of us was born in the past and grows older towards an unknown future which we imagine that we ourselves create. In the East, on the contrary, they tend to think of the future as flowing into a present and then passing into a passed time. But we do that also on occasion, and both concepts regard time as an objective factor, foreign to ourselves, to which we and events are inexorably subjected. One may note, however, that if we were in the stream of time we should not be aware that it was flowing unless we had at least one foot, so to speak, on the bank or unless observable events were stationary and untouched by the stream, which concept would separate us irrevocably from events.

It seems clear from all this that our notions of 'time' are vague and inconsequent to say the least.

Metaphysically, even philosophically, speaking it may now be noted that no such 'thing' as the 'past' can be said to exist otherwise than as a memory, always and inevitably incomplete and distorted at that, for whatever it may have been it has gone beyond recall and has never been as a 'past'. It might have been as a 'present', but what is that? Any event that was present in a time-sequence independent of ourselves as observers, is already in the supposed 'past' earlier in the time-sequence than we could have become aware of it, since the complicated process of perception via retina, chemical cellular changes, nerve impulses, further chemical cellular changes in the brain-matter, and psychological interpretation requires a lapse of time which must result in a 'time-lag' whereby a subsequent 'present' will have appeared by the time the previous 'present' has been perceived and conceived. Therefore no present can be known to exist; at most it might be maintained that an event which had once been present has subsequently been interpreted and recorded as having been observed. As for the future, we may imagine it, correctly or incorrectly, but we have no knowledge of it until it has become a 'past' which itself has been seen not to have any evidential existence.

It does not appear, therefore, that we have any evidence for the existence of such divisions as past, present and future, or that they exist at all otherwise than as conceptual interpretations of the notion of an objective 'time' that 'passes'. This conclusion is hardly original: Huang Po states that 'the past has not gone, the future has not yet come, the present is a fleeting moment', which may be said to imply what has just been elaborated.

May we not now just accept the conclusion of philosophers, from Heraclitus to Kant, who came to understand that no such thing as 'time' could have any objective existence?

Clearly it is a waste of time (this precious 'thing' we are dealing with!) discussing 'time' as an objective factor in our living, for it cannot possibly be such. If we wish to understand what it is we must look for its explanation nearer home. It must in fact be an aspect of whatever we ourselves are, and as such anyone who looks in the right direction, which is within, with a fasting mind, will immediately see that so it must be. Its aspect as a measurement of duration, based on astronomical factors, is artificial and secondary, and can henceforth be neglected, for that is entirely conceptual, as is also what is called 'psychological' or personal 'time', so that we are only concerned here with time as a synonym for duration.

As such it can readily be apprehended as the *active* counterpart of 'space' which is *static*, as a measurement thereof, that direction of measurement which measures volume in terms of duration.

As for 'space', that also is a concept based on measurement, on measurement in three directions—length, breadth, and height or depth, the three constituting volume. Volume is nothing but that, and 'space' is nothing but volume. Without volume 'space' is a term which can only imply vacuity, but vacuity as such is nothing but potential volume. The term as applied to a concept for that in which volume appears is a synonym for vacuity. Space, then, is also form, and form is nothing but three directions of measurement or volume, and we are incapable of cognising any further directions of measurement than the three which together constitute volume.

Therefore the perceptible universe, as far as we are concerned, is composed of nothing but the concepts which together appear to produce volume, which is space. But in order to perceive them at all, and so in order to perceive anything whatever, they must have duration. We also must have duration in order to perceive them, but what then is duration? We have just seen that duration is itself the *active* counterpart of space. Otherwise expressed, duration can be seen as a further spatial measurement, one that as such cannot be spatially interpreted by our senses, but only represented in the form of duration. This also is not original, for the concept of 'time' as the 'fourth dimension of space' has been played with by advanced physicists for nearly a generation. Physicists, the very eminent ones at least, have for some time been paddling on the borders of metaphysics, somewhat like children building sand-castles on the shores of the ocean. One day, no doubt, the in-coming tide will overtake them at their play, and they will be carried out to sea, where a few will drown and the others swim back triumphantly on the crest of the waves.

We must now ask ourselves whence come these measurements, the three which create the phenomenal universe which is composed of volume, and the fourth which is interpreted as duration. There can only be one answer, and that one very simple and very obvious. They come from the eye that is measuring. That eye is the centre of infinity, and infinity being in-finite, its centre is everywhere. In short that eye is just 'I', wherever, whenever, and whatever such 'I' may be.

I think it would be a pity to say any more: to draw conclusions is to force, or seek to force, an exposition down the throats of its hapless readers. What they may perchance seek has been offered, and they should be left to develop their own understanding of its significance. For such as may seek further indications, and without doing their thinking for them, one might add that the origin of 'time' has been brought right home to where it belongs. What then is 'time' and, to give it its conceptual totality, 'space-time'? 'What'? No, 'who', then, is space-time? Who, indeed.

II

The Incidence of Assuming Time to be Objective

SINCE NO phenomenon can be perceived without extension in space and in duration, if space and duration should have no objective existence no phenomenon could objectively be perceived, and if no perceiver can perceive without having the same spatial and temporal extension he could not objectively perceive. Therefore since no objective existence for the one can be established no objective existence for the other can be assumed either, and perceiver and perceived must be purely conceptual, i.e. existing only as images in mind.

This merely confirms the advaitic doctrine that objectivity is conceptual, that objects are void and have no nature of their own, and that their subject, as an autonomous entity, is as devoid of own-being or self-hood as they are. This, incidentally, is the burden of the Diamond Sutra.

It follows that every thought and every action which involves spatial and temporal extension is merely fabulous, as a dream is, for neither thinker, actor, thought nor deed, has any objective existence that is other than a concept in mind, again as it has in a dream. Spatial and temporal extension, therefore, being a description of the mechanism of manifestation itself, applies both to phenomenal perceiver and to what is phenomenally perceived, and must represent what we as sentient beings are, i.e. part and parcel of phenomenality itself whose only being is the noumenon which unmanifested it is.

This should convince us at least of the futility of whatever we do and whatever we say, taken seriously as demonstrations of autonomous individuality. If it does not enable us to apprehend that phenomenal performance as such is but a play performed by shadows, which after all is no more than the Diamond Sutra affirms and all the great Sages knew and told us, it is difficult to see what kind of demonstration could do so more effectively.

Are we not required clearly and profoundly to apperceive this phenomenal futility and thereby to apprehend that all that we are is the noumenality which enables us to apprehend at all as sentient beings, that, if you prefer, what we are is such apprehending, and that neither apprehenders nor anything apprehended can exist as such? For that surely is the answer.

73. *Ipse Dixit*

Where there is no extension in space and no duration in time there can be no self.

A 'self' is an imagined subject imagining itself as an object. While thus pretending to be an object it is posing as its own subject. And this mythical monster is extended in space and is dependent on duration.

Nothing spatial or temporal can have any but a mythical existence.

Is it not evident that at least, and also at most, each of us can see, and may say: 'What I am could not possibly be limited by any conceptual notion, spatial or temporal: in transcendence I am infinite and inherently I am intemporal!'

74. The Nature of Phenomena

I

TIME IS the serialisation of Intemporality. Therefore it is a sequential aspect of the intemporal, manifested as duration.

Regarding duration objectively, as a visualised concept, it has no significance other than as the temporal framework of the phenomenal universe. But, identified with what we are, it becomes thereby intemporality, its static aspect, so that we may know our own static aspect instead of merely our aspect in seriality. Identified with time we can ride into intemporality—where we belong.[1]

From what we have elaborated on the basis of time we can also see into the nature of phenomena, which are extended in space as well as in duration. Whatever could phenomena be but the spatially extended aspect of noumenality, sequentially manifested by duration?

We may very well know of our noumenality, that all we could ever be is what it is, but now we can understand the words of the Masters, and apprehend our phenomenality as the spatial extension of what each of us is as 'I', rendered cognisable by duration, and as a result of that the entire phenomenal universe, actual and potential.

For what is noumenal—noumenon and phenomenon being terms for two aspects of an indivisable non-entity—is potentially phenomenal, and what is phenomenal is noumenality rendered apparent.

We may ask, 'Could anything so simple and obvious be true?' The answer is in the affirmative, for it must necessarily be simple, and its truth is self-evident, for its truth and its simplicity both reside in the one word 'I', which is the only word which can define the source of every thing that appears to be, and which 'itself' cannot be any

---

[1] Intemporality and Time are rigorously inseparable, two aspects of the indivisible.

If we envisage 'Time' itself as an absolute, we find that its true sense is 'intemporality'.

thing. That one word must explain everything for, apart from it, no explanation could ever be possible.

Explanation requires a number of other words, representing concepts, such as noumenon and phenomenon, intemporality and time, infinity and the finite, but each is one of a pair of interdependent counterparts, indicating one aspect of the mechanism of manifestation, and every such pair in its mutual negation as a concept must so-negated remain as 'I'. That is all that 'simplicity' could be, as it is all that 'truth' is.

II

I DO NOT think that it can be maintained that save in its serial aspect sequential living could differ from non-sequential living, which is intemporal.

Living in a time-sequence brings into manifestation form in all its phenomenal aspects, and all categories of objectivisation, whereby it becomes objective living or living as our senses perceive it. Non-sequential 'living', on the other hand, knowing no dualism, devoid of subjects perceiving objects, is unmanifested.

To our conditioned manner of thinking as individual subject-objects the difference may appear to be absolute, and regarded phenomenally no doubt it is so, but it should be regarded non-dually and so-regarded no difference is apparent, since noumenally difference cannot be found other than in the seriality of the former mode of perception. Seriality, phenomenally cognised as duration, remains as a further measurement of space, and that alone may be supposed to constitute the difference. As such 'temporality', so interpreted, is revealed as being in fact the apparent 'difference', the 'difference' which itself causes the appearance of phenomena.

The further measurement of space which we know as time, being at right-angles to each of the three measurements of our phenomenal volume as each of these is to each other, then constitutes the super-volume which we sometimes refer to as noumenality, intemporality, or the kingdom of Heaven.

Note: Noumenal 'living' is, perhaps, not living at all? As, conditioned, we know it—perhaps: as Sages know it—perhaps not.

75. *The Pseudo-Mystery of Time*

APART FROM the obscure or ambiguous references to 'time' in the words of the Masters we have the observations of philosophers, often of great interest and perspicacity but always devoid of any satisfactory conclusion, whereas the comments of the unqualified amateur are superficial and contradictory. The reason for this morass, which explains nothing, is obvious: The two latter are applying to 'time' their conditioned technique of objectivising everything of which they treat, than which they know no other, whereas the former can only be understood by those who are able to perceive as they do, for never could understanding of what 'time' is be reached by envisaging it objectively, for it is not an object and there is exactly nothing objective about it whatever. What can be objectivised as 'time' is nothing of the kind, since there is no 'thing' there to objectivise. What is being objectivised is a concept—and no concept can reveal what 'time' denotes.

Let me refer to three well-known *wen-ta*[1] or parable-tales of the Masters. First the famous one about it not being the river that is 'flowing', but the bridge. The monk who understood was immediately awakened. The psychological reversion to thinking 'the other way round' readjusted his mind, restoring it to equilibrium, so that he saw that neither was 'flowing', that there was no such 'thing' as an objective flowing, that the apparent flowing was in his own mind.

Another Master pointed at a flock of wild-geese flying overhead, and his monk, having noted them, commented that 'now' they were 'gone'. This the Master contradicted, and enforced his contradiction by violently tweaking the monk's nose. The monk cried out with pain—and woke up! He too had reacted psychologically, reinforced by the physical shock, and suddenly perceived the Master's meaning, that the movement of the geese was in the monk's own mind.

A third is the equally famous tale of the sixth Patriarch, then an unknown monk, who overheard two monks arguing as to whether it was the wind or the flag which was in

[1] *mondo* in Japanese.

fact the cause of the apparent flapping. 'Neither', he observed, 'it is your mind'. They understood, and he was recognised as the missing Patriarch. In all these examples of movement it is the 'passage of time' which is in question. And the
monks were awakened precisely because subjugation to the
notion of 'time' is the mechanism of 'bondage'.

Let us essay a few remarks concerning this notion of
'time'. Time is envisaged as a straight line, though it might
be curved, and seems to resemble a great river. But if we
were in this river we could not be aware that it was flowing.
If it is perceived as flowing, that must mean that the experien-
cer is not within it. Therefore we are experiencing it from
outside 'time', and outside time denotes intemporality. Is it
not as simple as that? What we are cannot be 'in time',
since what is perceiving is not. We are, therefore, intemporal,
and intemporality is what we are. Only things phenomenal
are 'flowing' in the stream of 'time', only what we perceive,
what our senses tell us, including our phenomenal 'selves',
are temporal: what we are is immutable.

'Time', then, only seems to exist in mind, 'time' and
phenomena: they are conceptual objectivisations, among
them our own appearance and what we are conditioned to
suppose that we are. As *phenomena* we are 'time', 'flowing'
from birth to death, from appearance to disappearance, from
apparent integration to apparent disintegration, like every
'thing' else.

But 'time', like any concept, cannot have even a
conceptual existence without its interdependent counterpart,
which is 'no-time' or 'eternity'—and 'eternity' does *not*
mean ever*lasting* but just absence of 'time'. Interdependent
counterparts, as we know so well, have no separate existence:
they can never be 'one', but in mutual negation they are no
longer 'two' or apparently separate: they are reunited in
whole-mind as no-thing, as no object, as phenomenal
absence. Therefore 'time' and 'intemporality', phenomenally
conceived, are separate and opposites, polarised, but in the
mutual negation of non-phenomenality they remain as not-
different. In whole-mind they are reintegrated as wholeness.

It follows, and indeed we have already demonstrated
that it is so, that whereas phenomenally we appear to be

what 'time' is, noumenally or in whole-mind we are intemporality. What can we know of intemporality? Very little—which is why the words of the Masters are so obscure on the subject of 'time'. Phenomenally we can know nothing—for there is nothing therein of our kind of 'knowledge' to know. We can only point and indicate, as they did, for, after all we are trying to describe what we are, and 'I' cannot describe what 'I' am, since 'I' am rigorously no 'thing'.

Apart from the word 'I' we can all say that what we are is 'now', 'this' and 'here', the two latter being spatial concepts and the former temporal. Intemporally, then, we can say that 'I' am 'Now', for 'now' is not subject to time. In time we know no 'now', for the present is long passed before we can know it, and our 'present' is a reconstruction of a present that has already been replaced by another. 'Now' is 'vertical' and timeless whereas 'time' is 'horizontal': it is in another direction of measurement conceptually. 'Now' is eternal, that is intemporal. Our actions are performed in a supposed 'present', and what we perceive is in a supposed 'past', but *what* is looking is 'I' and *when* 'I' am looking is always 'Now', just as what is looking is always 'This' whereas what sees is a temporal 'that', and 'I' am looking from 'Here' whereas what is seeing is 'there'. Such phenomenal and dualistic concepts, if used with this understanding, can nevertheless enable us to apperceive what we are, which noumenally is Intemporality and phenomenally is Time.

Neither discursive reasoning nor dialectical analysis can ever reveal to us what these are, for they are what we are, and since what we are is devoid of objective existence what they are is so also. But we can apprehend what they are, and so what we are, and such apprehension is surely the essential element of liberation from our imaginary bondage. Why is that so? Well, because, when you come to think of it, is not that supposed bondage just bondage to the notion of supposed 'time'?

Note: Let us remember that in *time* we are also and simultaneously in the invisible dimension of *space* which 'time' represents to our senses—and that invisible dimension of space is called intemporality (which we cognise as time). Therefore in so far as we are temporal (or in temporality) we are also intemporal (or in intemporality).

76. *In Statu Aeternitatis*

I

WHAT WE ARE, what each sentient being is, as This-Here-Now, is intemporal I.

Being This, being Here, being Now, I am very present, in fact Presence itself, despite my total objective absence as 'I' which is my total presence as all phenomenal manifestation soever.

So I am not far to seek. In fact, being This-Here-Now, I am not to be sought at all, for I am present already, and who could there be to seek and who could there be to be found?

No seeker, no sought, no seeking, no finding—just I *in statu aeternitatis* where every sentient being appears.

II

I MANIFEST by dualistic polarity, by means of subject and object, negative and positive, a splitting of my Mind into opposites, without which the conceptual universe could not be manifest.

Thus I manifest as each object, and each sensorial object appears to function as a subject, but I alone am subjectivity and all functioning is my objectivisation in the world of appearance which is the Consciousness which I am.

III

BEING INTEMPORALITY as I, I manifest as time. Being Infinity as I, I manifest as space. Extended therein and measured from the ubiquitous centre of my intemporal infinity, all phenomenal aspects of what I am become sensorially perceptible.

Thus all manifestation, spatially and temporally perceived, is what I—This-Here-Now—am as infinity and as eternality, and I am all that it is.

Who am I? I have been given many names, but the oldest is TAO.

77. *Now*

Is IT conceivable that time could be stopped?
Conceivable but not possible.

Why is it not possible?
There is nothing to stop.

How so?
Only an object can be stopped, and time has no objective existence.

If time is purely psychological why does it not stop when we are asleep?
It is not purely psychological.

You mean that it is physical also?
Both psyche and soma are subject to temporality.

Why is that?
That is because time represents a spatial volume, a measurement of space that is interpreted as sequence. As 'space' time is fundamental.

Has 'space', then, no objective existence either?
None whatever.

But what is it as 'time'?
Intemporality.

Can it be seen as such?
The gap cannot be bridged conceptually, for there is a solution of continuity between opposites as long as reasoning is conducted dualistically, but an approach may be made in imagination.

How is that to be done?
Imagine the removal of the seriality of time, and what will be left?

Intempórality?

Yes, since time is seriality. Imagine the removal of immutability, and what will remain of the intemporal?

Serial time?

Quite so. In imagination you can at least see that negatively they have a common denominator.

Which is?

Presumably the spatial measurement which they represent, the one noumenally, the other phenomenally. Nevertheless it is only in their mutual negation that they reacquire that quality.

Does that *jeu d'imagination* help us?

Surely? Does it not show us that they are not separate, that time is an aspect of intemporality?

So what?

Since phenomenally we are sequential as 'time', so noumenally we must be immutable as 'intemporality'. Is that not the essential understanding?

Heavens, yes! Seen like that it is a demonstration at least of what we are!

If that needed proof would it not be that?

You said just now that the stoppage of time is conceivable: we can conceive it?

Of course: try.

Everything just stays put?

No, everything vanishes—including the conceiver.

Why is that?

Because time has no objective existence.

I don't see how that works.

You conceive time as stopping, but it is the conceiver that stops conceptually, since he is what sequential time is: seriality as such is conceived as ceasing—you and everything your senses report. 'You' cannot go on if time stops.

Which demonstrates that time is what phenomenally we are?

That it represents the seriality by means of which, alone, we can appear to be, and therefore is a measurement of what intemporally we are.

But does not that require that when we thus dis-appear we must automatically remain intemporally?

Excellent! Of course it does. That follows also from what we have just been discussing.

We are the one or the other, or both?

No, you cannot accurately say that!

Why not?

We are intemporal, intemporality if you wish, but what we seem to be temporally is just appearance.

Which is a conceptual existence, or pseudo-existence, manifested by means of the splitting of intemporal mind into subject and object, 'conceptuality' being comprehension by means of the comparison of opposites?

I think you put it clearly.

But are we not still in duality? Time and no-time are a pair of interdependent counterparts like any other.

Quite so. We must face up to that. But it is a verbal quibble. Time is sequence, sequence and the abolition of sequence constitute a measurement of 'space', a volume which includes the three-dimensional volume which our senses can interpret. That is only a geometrical concept itself, but these measurements all arise from one source, one 'eye' that is assumed to be measuring. What 'eye' is that, and where is it?

My guess is that it is my eye—if not 'all my eye'!

It is both! As a concept it is 'all my eye', but as a metaphysical truth it is my 'eye' as I.

And where is your 'eye' as you?

No, no! Now you are off the rails! It is MY eye, whoever says it, and every sentient being can say it—or if animals and plants cannot 'say' it they can know it without formulating it. Always it is 'I', and it is everywhere phenomenally.

Not a centre?

Yes, always a centre, wherever it is 'seeing from'.

How can that be?

I—or 'I-I', aham-aham, as Maharshi called it—is the centre of infinity, and the centre of infinity is necessarily everywhere phenomenally.

All that is conceptual.

Everything we say is conceptual. The trouble is that people are conditioned to accept conceptual objectivisation as what they call 'real'. But there is no 'reality'. All we can do, apart from the silent apprehension of the sages, whose apprehension cannot be transmitted, is to conceptualise it in an abstract form.

Yes, and what then?

Then we do what the Masters did, what Huang Po did.

What was that?

Destroy the concept. After a long and incredibly brilliant discourse on 'Mind', just as he was leaving the Hall he turned round and added, "And, by the way, please do not forget, there is of course no such thing as 'Mind' ", with which he disappeared leaving his monks bouche bée. Except, perhaps, just a few—for whom the whole discourse was given.

And we are among them. Which are we?

We are as well-qualified as they to be among the latter.

I am among the former—*bouche-bée!*

Not, I hope, when you read the discourse of Huang Po! That at least is clear.

Is it the shock of the exit that is effective?

As a shock—perhaps. But the point is that when the concept is abandoned, and however abandoned, the underlying truth remains—and should be evident.

Is it evident before the shock or after it?

There can only be one moment in time at which it becomes evident.

And which is that?

It is intemporal, but is represented in serial time by a moment.

Then when is it?

It is always, forever, everlasting—as well as being eternal. It is called NOW.

78. What Endures?

THE TERM 'duration', in English and in French *la durée*, habitually and conventionally implies 'lasting', that which endures in time, and it is idle and confusing to use words in another sense than that in which they are generally understood. Therefore this word is so-used in these Notes.

In fact, however, 'lasting' is an effect of sense perception, and has no factuality. Duration, in this sense, is an illusion occasioned by succession, so that succession can be said to be the mechanism of supposed duration.

But we are constitutionally unable to conceive events otherwise than in a context of duration, for timelessness, eternality, is inconceivable otherwise or in itself. Therefore the term 'duration' *should* imply timeless eternity as opposed to passing-time. That is to say, it should represent the measurement which can only be conceived as being at right-angles to seriality, the 'vertical' which cuts 'horizontal' time-sequence at every instant, and which 'endures' eternally in that dimension. Such endurance cannot be conceived by us otherwise than as 'lasting' in our time-illusion although such a concept flatly contradicts what essentially it should denote. In that sense, therefore, 'duration' describes intemporal eternality, a negative for which we have no positive other than the latin locution *Aeternitas*.

Expressed differently, what we imply by the word *prajnā* is eternal, is in intemporal duration, and manifests as function*ing* in the temporality of split-mind.

Why are we unable to conceive the intemporal? Must I give the answer to this vital query—the 'be-all and the end-all' of the whole subject? Is it not obvious? Is the answer too obvious to be seen? As a conceptual proposition it can be both seen and expressed—and in the shortest word in our language.

79. *Notes on Time*

EVERY ACTION we perform must accord with the future, with what is due to appear.

❖   ❖   ❖

It follows that whereas the present *appears* to exist but, as we have seen, is not known by us until it has become past, whole periods, let us call them aeons, are potentially existent at every moment of duration and must, inexorably, be 'lived'. It matters not whether we see them as 'past' rushing towards 'future' or as 'future' fading into 'past', our notion of living is a process of becoming conscious of them in a succession of moments which we know as 'existing' and the succession of which we think of as a 'life'.

Temporally regarded they appear successively, but though they may not exist before and after we experience them in the form of our experience of them, they are potential and inevitable and 'exist' intemporally *in statu aeternitatis*.

❖   ❖   ❖

To know that what you are is not subject to the concept of 'time', not just to know that it must be so but to be *aware that it is so*, constitutes liberation from all possible bondage.

Is bondage not bondage to time? Is the notion of 'time' not dependent on the notion of 'self'?

❖   ❖   ❖

We 'live' in a succession of temporal moments of what is intemporally an eternal present.

❖   ❖   ❖

We are living *in* history, not making it!

Probably there is no duration in the sense of immutability, but only in the sense of continuity.

But each moment must be eternal in another dimension at right angles to that of time.

❖   ❖   ❖

Living 'vertically', i.e. at right-angles to the 'horizontal'-living of sequential time, which may be seen as cutting across the latter at every successive instant, is noumenal living as opposed to phenomenal living, for that 'vertical' dimension represents super-volume, related to volume as that is to plane-surface.

The two have no common measure for the one has a further direction of measurement as a result of which it includes the lesser, so that what is experienced as successive in the latter is a totality in the former. 'Past' and 'future' must therefore be present and complete in the greater whereas in the lesser only a recent 'present' can ever be known except by memory and imagination.

❖   ❖   ❖

Time is seriality: Intemporality is simultaneity. Therefore we may well be living at all points of our 'life', past and future as well as the suppositional present, *now* and *always*.

❖   ❖   ❖

Our apparent or supposed existence, even if regarded as 'real', is nevertheless rigorously confined to moments only—those assumed to be the 'present'. These moments, successive in a time-context, are instantaneous impressions and have *neither consistence nor calculable duration*. Such 'existence' seems indeed somewhat 'theoretical', little more than a supposition?

❖   ❖   ❖

'He that does not see that time and space are fixed for us by the nature of our organs cannot move from the situation in which he is.'   (Maurice Nicol, *Living Time*)

Yes, indeed, but our organs are 'fixed for us' too. Time and space are interpretations of intemporality and infinity, and our organs are interpretations of that also. We are all in the same boat—except the mind of the skipper.

❖   ❖   ❖

Tied down to the dismal tram-line of our phenomenal lives, unable to take advantage of our innumerable opportunities, frustrated at every turn in the track to which, as chickens to a chalk-line, our beaks are held, *this is bondage*. Little wonder that we should want to be free, to be able to seize our opportunities, to fulfil our veritable destinies, and live as we know that we might live—and should. Are we not expiating a sentence pronounced by an unknown judge, instead of living in freedom which is fulfilment?

❖   ❖   ❖

Growth

A growing plant is the becoming visible in serial time of the totality (in 4 dimensions) of a plant. Or the passing through (3 dimensional space) of a quadri-dimensional object called by us a plant. Or the serial presentation called 'growth' of a 4-dimensional object in 3-dimensional space, apparently developing from what we regard as 'within'.

❖   ❖   ❖

(The present) NOW is never in passing-time. NOW is vertical, intemporal.

'Nothing ever IS in passing-time.' (Maurice Nicol, *Living Time*)

❖   ❖   ❖

What we know as 'time' is presumably the serial perception of a further spatial volume which our senses cannot spatially perceive as such, the which is Now or 'intemporality', and because it must be from Now that 'I' is perceiving.

❖   ❖   ❖

'Now' is not a moment of passing-time,

'Now' is immutable, eternal, and so also *forever* in Time.

❖   ❖   ❖

We live entirely in passed-time, for everything we experience has already happened before 'we' could become aware of it.

❖   ❖   ❖

In *time* we are also and simultaneously in the invisible dimension of *space* which time represents to our senses—and that invisible dimension of space is called intemporality (which we only cognise as time). Therefore in so far as we are temporal (or in temporality) we are also intemporal (or in intemporality). Therein we are whole: in 'time' we are bits and pieces.

The barrier between yesterday and to-day, or between to-day and tomorrow is imaginary; a life may be a totality, extended in the experiencing of it. May we not envisage it as a whole, live it not sectionally but totally?

A life need not be just a succession of conscious moments, each of which we live, and only thus, one after the other, like turning over the pages of a book. Noumenally we should be able to know our life as a whole?

If we know ourselves as Time this way of living becomes inevitable. Knowing ourselves as Time we begin to know ourselves as Intemporality, which is to say that knowing ourselves phenomenally we know ourselves also noumenally—for *they are not two.*

Knowing ourselves as Time we are knowing others as Time also; knowing Time to be timeless we know self to be selfless, and others vanish in our selflessness. That surely is noumenal living.

Knowing ourselves as Time takes us right out of temporality and carries us into the intemporal.

❖   ❖   ❖

Since we are all aspects of one another, serial aspects of what we all are, in order to judge one another must we not be failing lamentably to understand what that is?

❖   ❖   ❖

We seem only to live from moment to moment, a life of moments—only remembering the last and never knowing the next.

❖   ❖   ❖

'Forever' or 'everlasting' in Time is 'Now' in Intemporality.

'Now' is at the heart of things, i.e. the centre of eternity and infinity. We look at the universe from outside, Now sees it from within. That is what is meant by 'seeing things the other way round'. As 'Now' we are no longer helpless little lookers-on, we are at the helm. We no longer see the universe as 'the way it is, for good or ill', but as it must be—for we know that *we are manifesting it*, and that it is an objectivisation of what we are.

Eckhart said that the beginning of spirituality is dependent on recognising what one is as a being outside time.

❖   ❖   ❖

Nothing said in a time-context could possibly be true. So what?

In so far as we accept the serial aspect of time whatever we think and whatever we do must be subject to seriality, but to suppose that anything so presented could reveal the totality which anything veritable must necessarily be, is perhaps somewhat ingenuous?

What we perceive can be no more than a series of objectivised symbols representing something we never shall see because never could 'it' have objective existence.

❖   ❖   ❖

Nothing is in any direction of measurement, for all dimensions are This-Here-Now. They are measurements, within mind. They are an objectifying of what we are, *a measuring of objectification.*

❖   ❖   ❖

An 'I' existing in time, in succession, is nonsense *because* it appears serially: if it appears to have objective duration it must be imagined.

❖   ❖   ❖

Time, seen for what it is, undermines the 'self-nature' or 'reality' of every single thing on Earth.

❖   ❖   ❖

This which I am is the Source-Inconceivable, but it is the in-conceivability which in fact is what I am.

The sheer in-ability (to conceive what I am), not any 'conceiving' or 'non-conceiving', nor any 'it',

but just the not-being-able, it is, which reveals the sought that seeks vainly the sought

which is seeking.

❖   ❖   ❖

When the shadow of the ultimate object shall have disappeared, and nothing sensorially perceptible can be found, what then remains is what I am.

Since everything cognisable depends upon 'time' (the concept of serial duration), if that were excluded the entire phenomenal universe would cease to appear.

What would then remain? Surely all that could remain must necessarily be what was perceiving the vanished universe subject to 'time'.

Is not that precisely what we are all looking for?

80. *Bewildering Bits and Painful Pieces. IV*

CAUSATION EXISTS only in mind: it has no existence in the events which appear to depend upon it.

❧   ❧   ❧

When You Wake Up

You will stop traversing events, disguised as time, when you wake up: while others rush on. That is because you will have moved out of the apparent movement of seriality or sequential duration, and find that you are now Intemporality whose centre is ever I.

❧   ❧   ❧

Man conceives his Gods as composites of his 'selves', And he conceives them, not as intemporal but as everlasting. That is where he is wrong.

Gods are intemporal: and it is they who conceive man as lasting in time.

❧   ❧   ❧

Cut out the time-factor, abandon seriality, and where are you, who are you? You are Here! You are I!

❧   ❧   ❧

It is the seriality of time which 'creates' everything, causes everything to appear.

❧   ❧   ❧

Looking for a 'self' or 'what-we-are' is searching for something that isn't *there*.

Speaking of an 'ego' is speaking of something that isn't even *here*.

❧   ❧   ❧

Stop looking—and SEE!

PART V

ABSENCE

Each apparent individual may recognise that what he is can only be his absence as subject—as the total absence of his phenomenal subjectivity.

Is that not in fact the ultimate degree of understanding?

81. The 'Tenth Man' Story

YOU KNOW the quaint story of the ten monks travelling together from one Master to another, in search of the
enlightenment they had failed to obtain? Crossing a river
in flood, they were separated by the swift current, and when
they reached the other shore, they reassembled and one
counted the others to make sure that all were safely across.
Alas, he was only able to count nine brothers.

Each in turn counted the others, and each could only
count nine. As they were weeping and bewailing their drowned brother, a passing traveller on his way to the nearest town,
asked what their trouble was and, having counted them,
assured them that all ten were present. But each counted
again, and the traveller being unable to persuade them, left
them and went on his way.

Let *us* continue the story:
Then one monk went to the river-side in order to
wash his tear-stained face. As he leant over a rock above a
clear pool he started back and, rushing to his nine fellow-
monks, he announced that he had found their poor drowned
brother at the bottom of a pool. So each in turn went over
to the rock in question and, leaning over, looked into the
depths of the pool.

When all had seen their poor drowned brother,
whom, owing to the depth of the pool, they could not reach,
they celebrated a funeral service in his memory.

The passing traveller, returning from the town, asked
them what they were doing and, when he was told, pointed
out to them, and assured them, that since each had celebrated his own decease, and since all had celebrated the
decease of each, one and all they were well and truly dead.
On learning this each monk was instantly awakened, and
ten fully enlightened monks returned to their monastery to
the intense delight of their grandmotherly old Master.

Note: Each monk had found the answer to the *Open Secret*, which the
Traveller had missed because he did not know that it was a secret.
The Tenth Man is the only man: there is no other.

82. Source-Inconceivable

We are unable to conceive anything that does not 'last', including time itself. Conception, that which is conceived, is in total subjection to the concept of duration.

From this it follows that the act of conceiving must be outside time and that conception itself, therefore, is temporal.

What we are as 'conceiving' is thereby seen to be inconceivable, and inconceivability can be said to be a definition of This-which-we-are.

This-Here-Now, which is I, is inconceivable because it is intemporal and non-finite. 'Conceiving' cannot conceive 'conceiving', therefore since whatever is conceivable cannot be what we are, what is inconceivable must necessarily be the inconceivable that cannot conceive itself.

Therefore our very inability to conceive what we are may be apprehended as a direct expression of what-we-are, and perhaps the only one we can know.

83. Little Pigs

ALL OUR actions are serial, all our thoughts are serial, all our functions function in seriality: we neither know nor do anything that is not subject to the sequence of time. Even God, although called 'eternal', is seen as everlasting.

I think we have to admit that 'intemporality' itself, being a concept, is in fact thought of as enduring forever in time. The furthest we can go is to think of intemporality as 'outside time' or as 'timeless', but is not such a thought just a blank? And the next moment, and the next, we may think of it again; since it is 'still there', is still 'outside time' or 'timeless', we are unable not to think that it has 'lasted'. In fact, as 'duration', is the only manner in which we can conceive the absence of time as well as its presence. In the abstract, therefore, conceptually seen from a phenomenal centre, 'time' and 'timeless' are not different since both are subject to duration, whereas noumenally, on the contrary, they are also not different, and neither is subject to duration. In short, they are not different as regards what they are assumed to be, whatever that may be, their difference being in the fact that *both* are subject to duration phenomenally and to the absence of duration noumenally. But duration and non-duration are their only attributes; these are in fact all that they are or can be said to be.

We have already understood the reason for this, which is that the source of conceiving is not subject to the concept of 'time'; what is conceived is temporally conceived, so that every conception is temporal, but the conceiv*ing*, like all '-*ings*', is intemporal, is is-ness, is what we are, and so-being, cannot conceive the conceiv*ing* which has no objective quality which could be conceived as a phenomenal conception.

Does it not follow that whatever we may do phenomenally, in action or in thought, can never effect our noumenality? How could any deed or any concept reverse its temporal character which makes it what it appears to be? How could it remount the stream of 'time' and be retransformed from an objective concept into the intemporal subjectivity which it has never left? It must necessarily still be there, whatever it may be in appearance, since it is the source of conceiving. Sad as it may be to consider, we must nevertheless ask ourselves what on Earth all these good and earnest people think they are doing, practising this and that, some of them from morning to night? Perhaps they are becoming very worthy, even holy phenomena—but that is all, for phenomenalisation is one-way traffic. There is no such thing as noumenalisation.

Why is that? Presumably that is because what we are has never been anything but noumenal, which is intemporality, and what we appear to be is phenomenal, which is temporality, and phenomenality is the temporal aspect of noumenon, that is the serial aspect, for the reversal of which no mechanism is known or recorded or can readily even be imagined.

But what we can do, which is what we cannot not do, is to remain What-we-are—and to BE it.

Nothing we do in a time-context could have any noumenal significance, let alone be what we think of as 'true' or 'real'. No positive gesture or concept could effect noumenality. All we say and all we do and feel is confined to our own little dream-world of phenomenal nonsense.

That is why the negative way alone can help us, since it negates the positive, whereby—every positive impulse and concept being negated, or 'emptied' as it is called—our noumenality remains and is revealed.

And our supposed 'bondage', is it not bondage to all the conceptual rubbish in which we groutle from birth to death like piglets hunting for truffles? When we find one, is it not seized and taken from us at once?

84. I Am Only 'I' in Time

ONLY AS a sequence do we appear to exist,

And without succession in time there could not appear to be 'an I'.

The Buddhistic and Vedantic negation of a self *(anattā)* is automatically realised the moment the concept of seriality disappears.

That is why our phenomenal 'existence' is entirely dependent on the notion of 'time', in the absence of which what we are is necessarily intemporal and non-phenomenal.

85. Inside the Within

PERHAPS IT IS an error on the part of those who seek
to propound and to follow the Negative Way to place so
much emphasis on the pronoun 'I', which in its accepted
sense, to which we all are conditioned, initially implies an
objective 'self'? Does it not too readily allow the mere
transference of personal identity from phenomenality to
noumenality—even though we know intellectually that such
is neither intended nor possible? After all, or before all, it
is the notion of identity which constitutes the notion of
'bondage'!

What noumenally we are is basically a 'background',
the screen on to which phenomenality is projected, which is
an image suggested, I think, by Maharshi. The background
is essential, for without it there could be no appearance at
all, though where manifestation is concerned the 'background' itself is responsible for the appearance and is what
that is.

But it is the sense of 'withdrawal' which is needed, the
cutting out of all suggestion that the 'projected' appearance
is responsible for anything whatever. It is the 'background'
which 'withdraws' by taking back into itself the notion that
the manifestation it reveals has an identity of its own. No one
withdraws, and nothing is withdrawn: there is just a withdrawal. The disappearance of an illusory notion leaves things
as they are, as they always were and as they always will be,
in the total absence of the notion of 'time'. Action can only
appear to occur in a time-sequence, and where there is none
there can be no action. That is why the 'withdrawal' or the
'awakening' or whatever you may choose to call it involves
no action, since all action is phenomenal and temporal.

The image is sound also because 'mind' is the background of what we appear to be; as a concept it represents
that on which, or in which, we appear—perhaps better in
the Vedantic sense of 'Consciousness', other than which
there is nothing, though 'itself' is not anything objective.
Therefore 'background' implies foreground and indeed all
'ground'—although there is none. This also accords with
the famous 'mirror' metaphor for 'Mind': that which reflects

everything, retains nothing, and has no perceptible existence in itself.

The positive Way of Vedanta is essentially the proposition that 'I am I', whereas that of the Negative Way is 'I am not-I'. Both, of course, are equally true and equally false in themselves, but this 'withdrawal' into impersonality may lead more directly into the mutual annihilation of both truth and of falsehood.

The back of beyond is in front of ahead, and each is in front of and behind both itself and the other. What we are, therefore, is in another dimension altogether.

86. Love—and All That

IS NOT a sentence such as *L'amour véritable est impersonnel* (true love is impersonal) semantically very pure nonsense?

'Love' cannot have any conceptual existence other than as the interdependent counterpart of 'hate', experienced by A for B, the one a positive, the other a negative, reaction. Their resolution by mutual negation, the mutual negation of positive and negative superimposed, which 'impersonality' requires, leaves a conceptual inexistence which cannot be designated by the term for either counterpart.

Whatever is manifesting them dualistically cannot be any objectifiable 'thing', cannot be anything conceivable, since whatever it could be supposed to be, being noumenal, cannot have any objective or phenomenal quality whatever, and so should not even be referred to as 'it'.

What is thereby suggested noumenally can only be represented by the pronoun 'I', and any phenomenal expression or manifestation thereof other than 'love-hate' must need other terms. Nor can words such as 'bliss', 'felicity', 'benediction' and their counterparts, or even Sanscrit words such as *sat-chit-ānanda* or *karūna*, be adequate, even if preferable.

The conceptual expression of what is meant, which is an attempt to conceptualise an intuition, would need not a positive affective noun of any kind but, in an abstract intellectual context, an indicative *verbal* formulation suggesting non-objective relation. That, 'love-hate' could never achieve since it would constitute, manifestly, a contradiction in terms: what is impersonal could never be expressed by what is by definition personal. All this is an attempt to reach positivity by means of a positive—which is an example of self-elevation by means of one's own boot-straps.

Any attempt to express the non-objective in words other than the pronoun 'I', is inevitably impossible and so inevitably absurd. What we are seeking to express can only be what we are: being what we are, we can know it, but, being it, we cannot define it objectively, since 'I' can never define what I am, for I have no objective and so no objectivisable quality whatever.

If we absolutely must chatter about it, by pretending that 'it' is something objective, that is by making an image of it in order to shy coconuts or compliments at it, or if we cannot resist worshipping ourselves by worshipping it—which is what normally is the need we satisfy when we make high-falutin statements about pure, true, or divine love—would we not perhaps be better-advised to use some unpretentious technical term that is less flattering to our ego?

All that can be in question is a relation devoid of objectivity, whether it be applied to God or to the phenomenal universe—God here being necessarily objective and so phenomenal. There is no other 'impersonal' relation possible. But being non-objective it must necessarily be non-subjective also, i.e. if the object is not such, is abolished as such, the subject simultaneously ceases to be. What remains is 'I'.

The Christian St. John states that 'God is love':[1] since there can be no descriptive noun for it, it could hardly be said better, but does that mean that we are entitled to say it about ourselves? The experience itself reminds us of 'love'? Does it not remind us also of 'joy', of 'bliss', of Heaven only knows what else? But all are inadequate and wrong.

Why must we prattle about it at all? Cannot we be content to know it—when we can? Or are we so pleased with ourselves for having experienced it that we must at all costs let everyone know we have had it? If we *have* experienced it let us at least remember that all experience is necessarily phenomenal, and therefore that *what we are talking about cannot be 'it'*. Love, however ecstatic, is just affectivity. Love-hate can have no existence outside the dualistic universe of sense-perception and personal experience, and to seek positivity via a positive is indeed great folly.

---

[1] St. John explains the expression as follows, 'God is love, and he that dwelleth in love dwelleth in God, and God in him'. That is an indirect but *quite inescapable* way of saying that 'he' and 'God' have no objective relation. The Saint was also a Sage, and he knew what he was saying.

87. It May Be Suggested . . .

IT MAY BE suggested that awakening to what we are, or disidentification with a phenomenal object endowed with spurious subjectivity and freedom of action, can only occur as a result of a state of equilibrium between the positive and negative aspects of duality whose imbalance constitutes bondage.

In general the positive *(yang)* element is in excess of the negative *(yin)* element, for to this end are we conditioned from birth and by our unbalanced system of education. Religion tends to accentuate this imbalance, and thereby becomes an important factor in our bondage. The Negative Way of Ch'an-Taoism (and of Zen in Japan) almost alone systematically seeks to redress this imbalance, and that is the totality of method and practice in the pure forms of Ch'an, sometimes called 'the practice of non-practice'. If we study the ancient accounts of sudden awakening, which is the sole aim of the Supreme Vehicle *(Shresthyāna)*, I think we will find that this restoration of equilibrium is the factor which results in sudden liberation from supposed bondage—which seems to be a psychic inhibition—as it is the aim of the technique applied by the Masters.

The religious Ways are predominantly positive, or directly positive, seeking to reach pure positivity by cultivating positive affectivity—'love' of God, or of phenomenal objects, even of the universe as such—but the attainment of positivity by cultivating the positive can readily be recognised as a manifest absurdity like pulling oneself up by one's own boot-laces. Why is this so? It is so because objectified phenomenality is itself positive, and there is a solution of continuity between what phenomenally is either positive or negative and noumenality which is neither. Therefore 'liberation' is liberation from positive objectivity, and that cannot be achieved by any kind of positive or phenomenal activity. This I think, should be obvious? The technique of the Negative Way, on the other hand, consists in the systematic negation of every positive psychic activity, thereby rectifying the imbalance which holds us in bondage.

It may be suggested that we all have a craving for positivity, and that even the 'love of God' or the 'love of the

Lord', in Christianity and in Vedanta, is such. That may appear to us to be so, and it is certainly the cause of the apparently irresistible temptation to choose a positive—and so necessarily dualist—Way, but what we are seeking there is not ultimately, but only apparently, positivity. What we are seeking is our own noumenality, which although negative to us is neither positive nor negative, however it may appear to us, bound as we suppose ourselves to be, and so unable to apprehend that it is all that we are. This is, if you wish, the resultant of the mutual negation of the interdependent counterparts, positive and negative, and in order that such mutual negation may occur they must be accurately 'superimposed' like positive and negative films, for which they must necessarily be in perfect equilibrium. This will be found to be non-objective relation.

The mutual negation of all pairs of interdependent counterparts, of which positive and negative are the basic factors, is the result of compensation of the contrasting elements, light-and-shade for instance, each eliminating the other, leaving a blank which is known as the Void or, better, Voidness. But that is only *phenomenally* a blank, that is to say a total absence of conceptual objects. Thereby conceptuality is annihilated—and mind is rid of dualism and is 'made whole'.

What in fact results is what remains, which is what has always been, which is all that isness is, and that is what we are, all that we are, and there can only be one word for it, which is 'I'.

❖   ❖   ❖

The background of that metanoesis, of course, is the absence of phenomenal objectivisation, which constitutes appearance and whose only and apparent existence is in mind, manifested by the mechanism of supposed subjects and their objects. All this dreamed-stuff, as the Buddha called it in the Diamond Sutra, has cancelled itself out by the elimination of inferred subject/object. This has resulted from the equilibrium of the negative and positive *(yin* and *yang)* elements which rendered phenomenal manifestation possible for each and every apparent sentient being, whose sentient potentiality alone ever existed, expressed by the pronoun 'I'.

That, briefly, is the Way that is *Tao*, as its functioning is *Tĕ*, and he who understands it is a Man of Tao. It is also the in-forming element of Chinese Mahāyāna as represented by the Supreme Vehicle. Buddhistically expressed, the functioning is called *Prajñā* of which the static counterpart is *Dhyāna* whose dynamic aspect it is, terms which had a somewhat different connotation in the Indian Sanscrit vocabulary which translators still insist upon imposing upon Chinese scriptures, to our dismay, confusion, and general undoing.

This impossibility of reaching positivity via the positive is an illustration of Huang Po's frequent observation that Mind cannot be reached by mind, and the reason why an eye cannot see itself; it is why an 'I' cannot do that either, since it *is* itself, and a searcher cannot find himself, since the sought is the seeker. It is also, and particularly, why split-mind cannot see whole-mind, and why neither positive nor negative, divided, can see what they are beyond themselves, all of which are activities in which we are apt optimistically to engage, and all of which simply illustrate aspects of Huang Po's famous statement.

It would seem, therefore, that only by negating positive affectivity and positive conceptuality can equivalence be restored so that duality may be transcended. Noumenally all concepts are necessarily false, and nothing we can say in a serial time-context can be true. No affectivity can have existence outside the dualistic universe of sense-perception and personal experience, and to seek positivity via a positive is in itself great folly. Impersonality must be devoid of both elements, and can only be reached by total negation.

II

DIFFERENTLY SUGGESTED, and saying it rather than just reading it, negation is necessary because what-I-am is not any 'thing' sensorially cognisable, and in order that I may be aware of This-which-I-am I must cease to be conscious of That-which-I-am-not. Such a 'reorientation' of consciousness can only occur as a result of negating all the phenomenal attachments on which my false identity depends. Any and every positive thought or emotion must necessarily reaffirm my attachment to That-which-I-am-not, and positivity can only be cancelled out by negativity.

Therefore in order to rid myself of all my positive trammels I must bring my negativity into equilibrium with my positivity so that they may mutually compensate one another, the resultant of which must be the voidness of both positive and negative objectivity—which phenomenal voidness is what 'isness' is.

Ultimately, positivity is always affirmation of self, and negativity negation of self. And 'annihilation of the ego-sense is Liberation' *(Maharshi)*, is the burden of all the doctrines.

Positivity achieved can only lead to an affective phenomenon such as that holy monster (etymologically), a saint, as negativity achieved can only lead to an unholy monster, a devil, whereas equilibrium leads to a sage, who represents the perfection of normality. Can sages, then, not also be saints? Why, of course they can—sanctity, like devilry, is a phenomenon, and the phenomenal role of a sage can be demoniac as it can be saintly. This, also, was pointed out by Ramana Maharshi, than whom no one of our times has been in a position to speak with greater authority—since he was quite certainly himself a sage and was available to all comers for half-a-century. Although he had a background of Vedantic positivity his recorded statements were sometimes almost identical with those of the T'ang dynasty Masters of whom he is unlikely ever to have heard. Their words were not always reliably recorded, and are not often reliably translated, whereas his words were understood and recorded by ourselves. For that reason they constitute a precious cross-reference and confirmation.

Note: Only phenomenal objects can appear to experience, the sentience experienced is the nominative 'I' apparently experienced by the accusative 'me'. Experience (passing sensations) can only occur in a time-sequence, but the sentience experienced is itself intemporal.

There is no such object as sentience: it becomes a supposed object only when you think you are a being.

88. Who Are You?

WHO ARE you?
What I am is absence.

Absence of what?
Absence of myself.

So *that* absence, that *kind* of absence, is what you are?
No. What I am is total absence.

What do you mean by total absence?
Absence of the notion or cognition of absence-of-myself.

Why so?
Because cognition of my absence would imply presence of the cognition of my non-absence—which is not what-I-am.

So that you are then still present?
So that there would still remain 'myself' to be present or to be absent.

What, then, is your total absence?
Absence of the presence of absence-of-myself.

And who is there to cognise that?
There being nothing to be cognised, there cannot be a cogniser.

And yet there is that cognition so expressed.
There was a cognising, but no cogniser and no cognition cognised. Can you cognise that?

I can, but who, then, am I to do it?
Y o u are not at all, either. It is on account of total absence of absence that cognising can appear to occur. If there were any presence, even of absence, there could not be any cognising, or any phenomenon soever, for only out of absence as such can presence seem to be.

So that the Absolute, Tao, Buddha-mind, Godhead, Suchness, etc. are one and all just absence?
Each necessarily implies Absolute Absence, utter absence of absence as of presence, which is why anything at all can appear to exist.

Concepts, then, all concepts are total absence? But are the conceivers of concepts total absence also?

The conceivers of concepts are 'themselves' concepts, and nothing whatever but concepts.

So that total absence implies total absence of conceptuality?

Which necessarily requires the total absence of a conceiver of concepts.

Which I am?

Which you are not.

Which, as *what-I-am*, I neither am nor am not?

Yes, because the conceived is just the conceiver, and the conceiver is just the conceived.

Which objectively is no 'thing'?

Because subjectively it is no 'thing'.

So that is all that can be said?

What need could there be to say anything? The obvious needs no saying.

So that utter absence is obvious?

The utter absence of the source of conceptuality which is what all appearance is, is surely obvious? Patent, evident, inevitable?

❖   ❖   ❖

And I am that?

What you are can only be such and, being such, you are not.

And such is all that 'things' are, or can be *said* to be?

Is that not the final truth concerning what is neither true nor untrue, since no 'thing', true or untrue, has ever been or ever will be?

❖   ❖   ❖

Note: Phenomenally regarded, what I am is totally absent as appearance, since it is noumenal, and an absence comports also the absence of the subject of the absent object. Therefore my only presence is as all objective phenomena as such.

But, '*noumenally regarded*', what I am can neither be present nor absent, since nothing can have conceptual existence therein and so could not be cognised as either. But since noumenon cannot manifest directly as absence, direct noumenal manifestation must necessarily appear to be positive—and then it is presence, not a sensorially perceptible presence such as that of objective phenomena, but an immanent presence, ubiquitous and intemporal, total and absolute; and what-I-am, though phenomenally absent, is nevertheless absolute Presence.

It follows that total phenomenal absence is absolute noumenal presence, which is 'what-you-are'. And what is termed 'enlightenment' therefore, is *living* as what-you-are.

89. Time and Duration

PASSING-TIME is not different from duration, and duration is not different from eternity.

Passing denotes change: something changes. If there is no change no time has passed—which is immutability—for change is movement in space, and time is a measure of movement. Yet immutability, in order to be such, must endure in time.

Immutability, therefore, being absence of movement, is absence of change, absence of passing-time; and so it is duration. But duration 'lasts', and so it is subjected to passing-time.

Absence of change—immutability—is conceivable: absence of duration is not, for existence requires duration in order to exist, and duration requires existence in order to endure, so that the absence of the one requires the absence of the other. Duration and existence, therefore, are inseparable: if there is one there must be the other, they are aspects of one another, for without existence there can be no duration, and without duration no existence: they are dual aspects of *samsara*.

Absence of time, on the other hand, is incompatible with existence, and absence of existence is incompatible with time. Time, therefore, is seen as an aspect of phenomenality, and absence of time as an aspect of noumenality.

There can be no doubt whatever that what-we-are is a phenomenal absence, absence of time and of space, and to the presence of that absence, no name could ever be given, for any name, being a positive noun, must thereby return it to phenomenal presence which would leave it extended in space and in time.

Duration and non-duration cannot be different, for they must be two aspects of whatever they represent. Lasting is sequential in manifestation, and non-lasting is phenomenally not-existing, i.e. not enduring in sequential manifestation.

Non-duration, therefore, is the noumenal form of positive duration, that is to say its negative form which could never be perceived or conceived as a positive concept. It can only be referred to as isness, suchness, or just 'I'.

Timelessness is then seen as the noumenal aspect of Duration, and Duration as the phenomenal aspect of it.

90. Reality, What it is Said to Be

AN OBJECT is 'sensed', i.e. a perception occurs in mind: the notion of an object arises in mind, produced by stimulus and obtaining body from memory. Such is the genesis of a thought.

Then this impression is repeated again and again with incalculable rapidity until the impression assumes 'form' and is cognised as a 'table' or a 'star'. Each of these repetitions is a separate *quanta*, and the object is composed of these *quanta*, and so is built-up as a supposedly material unit. Such is the 'reality' of the object, and its dimensions, shape and distance are judged by these *quanta*, the quanta being attributed to the light by which the object is perceived, whereas they lie exclusively in the perceiving mind.[1]

All light being presumed *quanta*, all distance is presumed *quanta*, and all velocity, and all are only in the observing mind. All, therefore, depend upon succession, the sequence of time, which itself is nothing but seriality—the repetition of *quanta*.

It must follow that the most 'distant' star is neither further nor nearer than the nearest, for all these calculations are based on false premises and are purely imaginary—images in mind. Such is the world of form, the material universe that science observes and studies with such assiduity —and all is devoid of existence outside the scientist's own aspect of mind. In studying nature he is studying a space-time creation which is ultimately his own creation and so is himself.

I have presented the case as clearly as I could, and express no opinion concerning it. It would appear that the greater physicists—such as Einstein, Jeans, Eddington, Schrödinger, all arrived at some such conception, or left words from which it can be deduced. It is also congruous

---

[1] It was pointed out in Ch. 51 that since the velocity of light is unaffected by the motion of an observer, approaching its source or receding from it, light must manifest the further direction of measurement (dimension) from which the observer as such must be looking. This confirms, and is confirmed by, what is stated here regarding *quanta*.

with the implications of some of the Sutras attributed to the Buddha.

Thus 'time' is mind's *repetitive* manifestation, and is composed entirely of these *repetitions* which constitute a succession of *quanta*. Such *quanta* have no independent existence as such, that is they are conceptual only, images, laboratory apparatus, and 'time'—their resulting concept— has no factual existence either, since both merely represent the sentient mind or supposed 'ego'.

The least satisfactory part of this thesis is the genesis of the original perception which to my understanding could only be a concept, i.e. a *pre*-concept.

91. As Science Sees It

WE ONLY see a star once at a time: we then repeat the experience in our minds indefinitely, and so give its light, and all light, a potential velocity, and the star a potential distance in what we term 'light-years'. But the repetition in mind consists of so-many *quanta*, and we say that light moves by *quanta*, even that it is *quanta*, but the *quanta* are the repetitions in our mind, not in the light, so that the velocity, the distance, and the light itself seem to have been found to be all in our own mind.

If this is not an accurate description of the latest findings of physics, as I believe to be the case, it should be an accurate description of what metaphysics has understood, believes and should teach.

Each original perception remains unexplained herein, but it is evidently only an image, with a mnemonic background which arises in mind itself, other than which there is nothing for it to be in the supposed Cosmos.

For all phenomena are totally conceptual.

Note: All perception is thus, by *quanta* in mind, so that motion is a relation between subject (thereby become an object) and its object, and nothing moves ('movement' being only a succession [of *quanta*] in 'mind'). 'Passing time' is a calculation of the *quanta* of perceptive repetition within mind, and 'distance' a calculation based on 'time'.

Thus there is seen to be no 'time', no 'distance', no 'velocity', and so no 'space'. Space-time is revealed and demonstrated as the aspect of 'mind' with which we are identified as supposed individuals.

92. *The First and Last Illusion*

PEOPLE, INTELLIGENT people also, laugh at the idea that there is no such thing as a self, whereas to us it is quite obvious. Why is that?
It is because they are conditioned to imagine self as an object, and all objects appear to exist.

Why cannot they see that self could not be an object?
Seeing that is inseeing, and they are only conditioned to outseeing.

But it is also a valid logical proposition.
Quite so; can you not so put it to them?

I have never tried. Why is there no self?
If you look carefully you will find that you cannot think of what you are.

Can I not?
You cannot.

Why?
Because what is thinking is what you are.

Does that make it impossible?
It does. You can only think of an object: what is thinking is subject. Therefore thinking cannot think of what is thinking.

In fact subject cannot cognise itself?
Whatever is perceived, whatever is thought of, is an object. In order to perceive or to cognise your self you would have to be an object. When thinking, perceiving, cognising, you are the thinking, perceiving, cognising—not an objective image in mind.

You mean that it cannot be *said*, for instance, because it is itself which is *doing* the saying, or thought of because it is always what is thinking the thought; nor can it be seen because it is inevitably what is looking; nor be an object of knowledge because itself is what is cognising?
It cannot be thought of because 'it' is what is thinking that thought. How, then, could there be 'a self', which is necessarily an object? Is not such a 'thing' unthinkable? How could it be possible? An object cannot be its own subject!

You mean that there never has been a self?
Never. Never has been, is not, and never will be. It is an utter impossibility, a pre-post-erous contradiction in terms.

But cannot I be both?
Both subject and object?

Yes, one after the other.
You would then be two separate and consecutive objects. There is no sequence except in illusory 'time'. What we are is not so limited. Only a concept is dualistically bound. What we are is not a concept; that is the condition of appearance only.

But cannot I see your self, and you mine?
Indeed no. Anything either of us can see must necessarily be an object. 'Self' is what looks, not what is seen. And 'self' is singular, not plural.

You mean that self always remains subject?
There is no self to 'remain'. There is only a functioning: even if functioning could ever be anything else it could never have been self. The term has no other meaning.

Then what is the subject of the object that I mistook for self?
Why, self of course. There is no other subject. Always and everywhere. Just self—written with a capital letter in translations from the Sanscrit.

The name for you, for me, and for. . . .
The beetle. Yes, of course. There is only one, and 'it' is no 'one'.

Then what on Earth can 'it' be?
'It' is not on Earth; 'it' produces the Earth by means of 'its' functioning. 'It' is all that any and all of us are, ever were, and forever will be.

That means that 'it' is eternal?
There is no 'it' to be eternal or not-eternal, temporal or intemporal, finite or infinite. But what they are is precisely what 'it' is.

And what are we?
What 'it' is—we are. What else could we be?

But that is no 'thing'!
No 'thing' whatever—for no 'thing' ever was, is, or ever will be.

How can we say that?
Because there is no time, nor space, other than as the extension of images in mind.

Images of what?
Images of what we are as self, objectified as what we appear to be and are conditioned to believe is what we call 'ourselves' and all that we cognise.

Is that your whole doctrine?
What do you mean? Who am I to have a doctrine? It is what all the Prophets have seen, what all the Teachers have taught.

But they don't tell us all that!
You mean they don't express it in that way?

Surely not.
They express it in accordance with the understanding or mental conditioning of those among whom they lived.

Which is very different from ours, of course?
And from that of one another, geographically, demographically, and chronologically.

And those are not suitable for us?
We try, try very hard, to understand it as they propounded it for their contemporaries, but we find it a very long and arduous process which involves an acquiring of the essentials of their conditioning. Few of us succeed.

So that we should find this modern Western idiom easier?
Our own conditioning has to be overcome, or undone, demolished before we can apprehend it; that alone is a long and hard task, and one that is longer and harder than theirs was in their day and place, for they were less rigidly conditioned to materialism than we are. To acquire an apprehension of theirs as well, with its complicated religious background, is rather too much for most of us, and there is no reason to suppose that we are more fitted for the task than they were.

Then religion is an obstacle?
It is both a Way and an obstacle.

How is that so?
As a Way it is traditional, but devotion is emotional and positive, and affectivity is as great an obstacle as intellectuality—for both are turning away from ourselves—the true 'Within' of Jesus—towards an Object, towards 'other', towards objectification of all thought.

In worshipping 'other' is one not worshipping his 'self'?
He is, but unless that is understood he is still in the dark and does not know what he is doing. In any case both affectivity and dialectics are outflowing.

Because they are positive?
Exactly. Only via constant and total negation of all that is positive, of all conceptual so-called 'reality', of all that is phenomenal, can noumenality which—necessarily and evidently must be all that we are—be clearly apprehended.

And such apprehension should be perfect understanding of our relation to the universe, and realisation of what we are?
Such apprehension is preliminary understanding, if you wish: perfect understanding is the living of what has been understood.

And how is that to be achieved?
It cannot be achieved. It is not an achievement.

Why is that?
Why? Because it is the final understanding that there can be no one to achieve anything, and no thing to be achieved.

Who, then, can do it if we cannot?
Whoever are 'we', and who is there to do what or look for whom?

Our self? Is it not our self that we must find?
Is not that like ringing for someone who is already in the room?

But surely we must find what enables us to see?
Is not that like looking for spectacles that are on your nose and without which you could not see spectacles?

At any rate it is I who am looking for myself?

If you dial your own number on the telephone, will you get the connection?

Then we must look in another direction?

Will you see what you are looking for by looking in the wrong direction?

Of course not! I mean by looking in the *right* direction!

You will not see it even then.

Well, how on Earth . . .?

No amount of looking in any direction could help you to see what is looking.

93. We Speaking—Phenomenally

1.   WE ARE what sentience is, and we do not know what sentience could be other than our psycho-physical apparatus which experiences it.

We are the presence of what we appear to be; what each of us appears to be is his presence, and what dualistically (as an object of subject) we imagine each of us to be is other than what each other of us is.

We are presence, therefore presence of an absence that we know must necessarily exist as counterpart of our presence, but which we are unable to perceive and of which we know nothing. Therefore we know our absence as Void.

2.   That is why we sentient beings are everything we can know, and how we must be everything, because without our presence nothing whatever could be seen or known.

We are manifest, but how or why such manifestation occurs we do not know.

3.   Our functioning, though apparent, is inexplicable, but it has been called *prajñā*, of which the static aspect has been called *dhyāna*. But we are unable to imagine what kind of 'thing' this could be.

What we are is different from what everything else is, and everything is different from what we are. Therefore we are all separate beings or things.

4.   This is how we are, but we do not know why, nor whence we derive, except that we think it must be from God.

We cannot find or know what we are, for we are merely present, and our presence is all that we seem to be.

5.   Looking for ourselves is finding our presence. There is some thing sought and someone seeking, some thing seen and someone looking, because what is sought for is the presence of someone acting, and what is seen is the presence of someone seeing.

6.   All this can be said and known by us because objects are the presence of the objects of subjects that are present, presence itself being the presence of objects, and absence their absence. Whatever is present is positive, and is the

absence of whatever is negative—and such is What We think that we Are.

7.   That is how we sentient beings see and know every-thing that 'is', how everything 'is', and why all that we 'are' is what our sentience reports via our senses.

Note: Did the implication of par. 3 of No. 1 above reach the bull's eye? We are conditioned to think of 'absence' not only as of what is not here or not there but also as of what is not anywhere, of pure vacuous not-ness, the void of annihilation, despite being told by the Masters that the Void is a Plenum. Here our presence is presented as the persona or mask of what, *of all* that, we truly are—which is what lies behind that persona or appear-ance. Behind a Greek mask lay an actor: the mask was appearance, phenomenon only, all else lay behind, invisible. About one-seventh of an iceberg is visible, six-sevenths lies hidden beneath the surface. What is apparent is positive and present, what is not apparent is negative and absent.

Always it is the non-apparent that matters most, always the phenomenal is merely an appearance of what lies behind it. The negative, the noumenal is the source, origin, substance (*sub-stance :* what stands beneath); and the positive is the surface appearance. There could not *be* anything but Absence. Always Absence—that which negates the superficial, the positive and present and phenomenal—is what IS, i.e. what every sentient being may say in the words I Am This I Am.

The supreme error consists in mistaking positivity for all that is.

94. I Speaking—Noumenally

1. I AM TOTAL absence of sentience, so that sentience may be.

I am the absence of whatever may appear to be, and whatever may appear, I am its absence, and what it is.

I am absence of presence, so that presence may be.

2. That is why I am everything, and how I am everything, because without my absence nothing whatever could appear.

I am unmanifest, so that manifestation may be manifested. Manifestation is entirely my non-manifestation.

3. Functioning is my non-functioning, just as *prajñā* is *dhyāna*, and my non-functioning is functioning, just as *dhyāna* is *prajñā*.

What-I-am-not is what everything is, and everything is what-I-am-not. Therefore we are not separate.

4. This is how I am not, and why everything appears.

It is also why I cannot find myself, or know myself, for I am my absence; it is my own absence *That I Am.*

5. Looking for me, looking for looking, is *finding* my absence.

The sought is the seeker, what is seen is the see-er, because the sought is the absence of the presence of the seeker, and the seen is the presence of the absence of the see-er.

6. This is all that can be said or known, for what is objective is the presence of the absence of subject, presence the presence of the absence of objectivity, and positive is the presence of the absence of negativity—for such is *That I Am.*

7. This is why I am everything and yet am no thing, why everything neither is nor is not, and why all that we are is I.

95. *Absence*

PRESENCE IS no thing: Absence is all.

Presence is appearance: Absence is the source of everything.

Presence is what is not: Absence is what is.

For phenomenal absence is noumenal presence.

What I am is phenomenally absent: it is the phenomenal absence of My presence.

Every time I say 'I' Absence is speaking via presence.

I am Absolute Absence—absence of presence and of positivity.

Absolute Absence is absence of me—of all my phenomenality.

So I am the absence of my self, and the presence of Absence.

What I am is the absence of everything I appear to be and can think that I am.

What I am is the absence of all presence.

As Absence, I am always 'the Tenth Man'.

The Tenth Man

What I am is the Absence of my presence.

My presence is a dualistic mechanism of subject-object, of negative-positive, like the escapement of a clock, manifested phenomenally and dominated by a positive I-concept—the whole purely conceptual, composed of concepts arising as a result of sense-perceptions.

The noumenal absence of my phenomenal presence, which is also the noumenal presence of my phenomenal absence, is what I am, and of every pair of interdependent counterparts it is *neither* (the one) *nor* (the other), and the total negation of each and every concept of which phenomena are constituted.

In this phenomenal absence which I am, there is no time, either positive (temporality) or negative (intemporality), for there is no thing therein to be extended or not-extended in space-time. And I am only awareness of NOW.

Being unmanifested as what I am, my Absence knows neither affectivity nor intellectuality, which are manifested by my presence. This Absence is *Void*, and it has also been called *sat-chit-ānanda*.

It is my Absence which is meant when I say 'I Am This I Am'.

❖ ❖ ❖

We must BE our own Absence in order to manifest a spontaneous non-volitional Presence. (We must be 'absent' in order that 'present' may be.) Effectively in order to be *'present'* we must be *'Absent'*. But where we are and when we are is neither present nor absent, and what we are is neither presence nor absence, but the mutual negation of both. That is to say that neither concept is applicable, nor is any pronoun. Why? Because all words signify what is objective— and what we are has no objective quality and so cannot be objectified at all.

Our cognisable presence or absence can only be an objective, and so phenomenal, presence or absence—and therefore cannot be what we are. Noumenally, then, what we are is neither, but phenomenally regarded it can be conceived as the one or the other, but not both. By definition it must be absent, but it can be presence as appearance.

96. Death

DYING IS dying to the future, rather than to the past.
We could die to the past without any very serious qualms.
It is the prospect of there not being any more foreseeable
future which 'puts the wind up' us. Quite a number of us could
bear the prospect of foregoing the future, even so, if it were
not for the generally rather painful character of the process
of dying, including the accompanying hypocrisy, secrecy,
lamentation (real and assumed) and the technical impedi-
ments that prolong it.

Even that only applies to those who assume that there
is something living that could die, and that such is what they
happen to be. But is there?

The only answer to that query is to look and see. And
if you can find anything of the kind, please to let me know.
In order to die, that which dies must have been born, and
for that to be anything that matters it must be an entity.
But only matter appears to be born, only matter appears to
die, and matter just doesn't matter very much, does it?

If you were to ask someone whether he had been born,
he would probably laugh, and if anyone were to ask whether
he would die, he might cry. But that one could hardly have
looked into the matter very closely; if he had he would have
apperceived that no entity could be born, had ever been born
or ever would be, could ever die, ever had or ever would die.
Only energised matter suffers that sort of thing. So what?

So what? Let us attend our own funeral, of course?
Alas, fun though it sounds, not being entities—since there
are none—we could hardly do that. No, being what we are,
devoid of any trace-element of objectivity, we will just go
on with our job of manifestation—quite impersonally as
usual. There is plenty of matter left to keep us busy playing
the game of living.

97. *The Bubble of Bondage*

OBSERVE EACH of your performances from waking to sleeping, and from sleeping to waking: is not your every action a reaction? Are you ever not-conforming to conditioning, to precedent causes, called 'habits', fashion, or anything else?

Have you ever been free?
So how could you be bound?

Examine what you regard as your self: can you locate any entity anywhere that could be subject to bondage?
Have you ever been bound?
So how could you be free?

Does this way of seeing liberate from bondage to the notion of being bound?

Note: In case it should be necessary to state—there cannot be any such condition as 'bondage' without a corresponding condition of 'freedom', nor one of 'freedom' without 'bondage'.

Isness

FREEDOM IS not freedom from any thing.
Bondage is not bondage to any thing.

It is not even a question as to whether there is or is not any thing to be bound or to be free.

The truth about problems is not whether some thing is or is not so.

The truth about questions is not whether this or that is right or wrong.

There are no questions.
There are no problems.
There is no freedom or bondage.

Such is noumenal understanding—for there is no Time.

98. *Absolute Absence*

WORRIED ABOUT something?
Yes, what I am. Do you happen to know?

Of course I do.
Well, what am I?

My absence. What else could you be?
Y o u r absence?

Evidently.
But here you are, present, and evident.

You are speaking as a shadow, a reflection, a bubble. . . .
Yes, yes, I've read the Diamond Sutra, also.

When people who have understanding happen to ask questions
the least one can do is to reply from the Prince-Host-
Principal position, not from that of the minister-guest-
function. We have an obligation at least to do that.
Very well, but what has your absence got to do with it?

My absence is what you are.
Then what is your presence?

My presence you can see, hear, touch—whenever you feel so
inclined.
*You mean that your absence as a phenomenal object accounts
for all phenomenal presence, including mine?*

You have come-to at last. Yes, yours and the beetle's, the
elephant's, the sparrow's, the seal's, and my own as a
phenomenal object.
You must all have a potent kind of absence, old man!

All possible potency must lie in its non-manifestation.
Why so?

Where else could it lie? Can manifestation produce manifestation? Can potency produce potency? Can presence produce
presence?
*I suppose not. Why should anything so obvious be ignored?
Why could I not think that up for myself?*

Because, like many other people, you are still just a trifle too rigorously conditioned to looking in the opposite and wrong direction! Also, although when expressed it has become a thought, in itself it is not such but just being aware of what is, or of how things are.

Sounds as though it might be important. Is it?

Every understanding is important. 'Understanding one thing, you understand all'—as several of the greatest Masters asserted. I can say at least that thoroughly to understand this is in itself to understand the little that I understand.

I can insee that it must necessarily be so, but I become muddled when I start to think about it.

Is not that because you look in the wrong direction and think, instead of looking in the right direction and insee? Are you not looking phenomenally instead of noumenally, as minister-guest-function instead of as Prince-Host-Principal? From that point of view you can only see goods and chattels.

Can I do anything about that?

You can. It is one of the things you can do.

I confuse the ordinary mundane and phenomenal stand-point with the noumenal point of view?

We all do, but it is an essential discrimination, *the* essential discrimination. Only Sages can allow themselves to ignore that illusory difference.

To them that difference does not exist?

There is no difference between Yes and No. Every statement is necessarily true and false both ways.

By which you mean that positive and negative, and all opposites, are one to them?

No, not one. But they both mean the same thing in their mind. Have you never experienced it yourself?

As a matter of fact and now that you mention it—I have, and to my great surprise!

Good! And don't discourage it! If any kind of practice could be helpful that one might well be.

It implies that understanding is there already and is mutual?

That may well be so.

Then, sagely speaking, what we all a r e is our phenomenal absence?

Perfect, to my ear.

So that Absence as such is the cause and origin of all presence?

Presence being appearance in a time-sequence.

Come to think of it, there could not be any such thing as being present if that thing could not also be absent. But could it not be absent here and present elsewhere?

It is; necessarily it must be. But then the 'where' is still 'here'.

I mean, apart from being round the corner or in Australia, where can it be?

Here, of course. But your question was phenomenal; in that optic being elsewhere is still presence; that is only absence to an individual spectator. But Absence as such is total absence—absence of phenomenal absence as well as of phenomenal presence.

Good, that one I can see. Total absence is transcendent?

'Transcendent' is a positive term which suggests the maintenance of a positive identity else*where*. But there is no 'where', nor any 'when', and least of all a 'what'. My Absence, absence as 'I', implies non-entity as phenomenon and non-entity as noumenon. Only Such could manifest at all.

Do you not mean that only a s Such could I manifest at all?

Quite so, you are correct; I was in error.

You said it on purpose to test me!

Not at all, I was just plain wrong. What matters is that you understood nevertheless.

I can see clearly that Absence could not be any absent thing or object that happened not to be present in the sense of being sensorially perceptible. But then what is it?

The utter absence of realness or thingness—of any sensorially perceptible or mentally conceivable object.

And Such is my Absence?

Such is Absence (lamentably referred to as 'Reality'—since that means thingness—the most unsuitable and probably the most inapposite word in the language). Such is all absence, absence of whatever appears and is assumed to be.
Am I unique in feeling a trifle lonely as 'total absence'?

Like an astronaut left behind in solitary circuit going round and round forever in cosmic space?
Yes, just like that!

Is it possible that you, of all people on this Earth, could be such an ass?
It is, but why?

Because my dear good chap, it is being God.
A lonely and tedious job, if ever there was one. Wouldn't take it on at any price.

Perhaps I should have used the impersonal term 'Godhead'.
Were you counting on the shock? Godhead still sounds a trifle isolated and diffuse. Tenuous and unsubstantial at least; something rather like a huge sponge!

It is not objectifiable, being the source of all objectivity. It cannot, therefore be described, but the Vedantists call it *sat-chit-ānanda*—which implies some such notions as 'being-consciousness-bliss'.
The two first sound familiar, the latter like one of the drugs these young men and women are said to live on nowadays. 'Absence' does not make my heart grow fonder.

People have always wanted something positive—joy instead of sorrow, pleasure instead of pain, bliss instead of misery, but what nonsense that is! The Buddha saw the suffering, but no one knew better than he that there is no suffering without its opposite.
So what was he up to?

Exactly what he declared: the abolition of suffering.
Which meant the abolition of joy?

Inevitably.
And so—what?

'*Absence*' means what it says.
And what is that?

Absence of everything—including affectivity.
So that this 'bliss' and 'joy' and 'light', and all the rest of it is 'all my eye'?

There is no entity to have an eye, not even a pseudo-entity. Awakening to Absolute Absence is integrally without 'ens'. How could it be imagined? If it were 'blissful' there would have to be 'blisslessness'—and an entity to experience both.
So they have all been pulling our legs?

They have been playing up to the universal craving for positivity as opposed to negativity, as they nearly all do except the Ch'an Masters.
So what can it be? To what does one awaken?

To Absolute Absence.
And what does that feel like?

My dear chap—there is no one to feel anything, and nothing to feel anything with! How or what could there be? Think for yourself. Insee for yourself.
I still ask for an answer. Every sentient being on Earth would do the same.

My answer is no better than yours, not one whit.
Give it me nevertheless.

The 'abolition of suffering', propounded by the Buddha, includes also negative suffering.
What is that?

'Suffering' not positively recognised as such.
Is there any?

Of course there is.
How do you know it?

Take the weight of your body. Do you cognise that as suffering?
No.

If you were suddenly relieved of that would it not be the disappearance of a burden, a phenomenon made absent? Is that not why you enjoy bathing, particularly in salt water?
Yes, I suppose it would be a relief.

Phenomenal living *as such* may well be a heavy but unconscious burden. Living in sequential time comprises painful memories, remorse, regrets, as well as fears of the future, of pain, loss and death, and, apart from apparently present pain and worry, may constitute a heavy load of unrealised and negative suffering, to which we are so used that it is not experienced positively as such.
You mean that the taking-out-of-appearance of both positive and negative suffering must result in joy?

I mean rather that the *re-establishment of a norm*, of which we can know nothing now, may be assumed, and that norm may be something which, if we could experience it, might seem to *us* to be intense delight and supreme happiness.
You think that may be it?

That at least would explain the serenity and delight of which the *jivan-mukta* speak.
When they are still in the dualistic dream-phantasy?

There cannot be positive joy if there is no longer positive suffering, but the removal of both positive and negative suffering must surely restore a norm which is a condition corresponding to what we can imagine as serenity, which is unknown to us, and which we vaguely think of as 'joy'.
It should be just serenity, perfect serenity, but to us it must be i m a g i n e d as pure joy? Having no cares, no worries of any kind, alone should constitute joy!

Serenity is not altogether incompatible with Absence. But Absence means what it says.
And what is that?

Absence is, quite simply, absence of self.

99. *A Dieu*

So MANY people searching—searching for what?
A self? But there isn't one! No such 'thing' exists, has ever existed, or ever could exist.

Why? Because it would need another to find the one.
They are searching for themselves: how could anyone find himself?

> That is all there is in it.
> That is the Big Joke,
> And why it is a big joke!
> And why there is nothing more to be said.[1]

Note: These few very ordinary words may mean little to you. That I know well: in which case please accept my apologies. But I also know that they could mean a very great deal indeed; in that case perhaps you will do me the honour of accepting them?

[1] Oh, by the way, there is something that *has* been said; did you notice it? 'Looking for me, looking for looking, *is* finding my absence.'

100. Bewildering Bits and Painful Pieces. V

'EMPTINESS' IS absence of anything or anyone to be 'empty'. (As long as there is someone to *crave* there will be craving, etc., etc.)

❧   ❧   ❧

Absence of absence is the essential absence: it represents a further dimension of absence.

It is the absence of that absence which is absence of presence.

❧   ❧   ❧

The absence of (the concept of) 'the absence of presence and absence', or the absence of the concept of 'neither presence nor absence', was Vimalakirti's definition of non-dualism (see HUI HAI, p. 111, and n.132).

That is the absence of the concept of 'neither . . . nor . . .' or Absence of (that kind of existence which is) non-existence.

❧   ❧   ❧

Noumenon is ubiquitous, all pervading; there cannot be anywhere in which it is not, nor any moment at which it is not present.

But itself also is not.

❧   ❧   ❧

We need not only phenomenal absence in order to cognise noumenal presence, and phenomenal presence in order to cognise noumenal absence.

But the absence of both phenomenal absence and of noumenal presence if we would cognise what we are.

❧   ❧   ❧

Empty

A Ch'an Abbot said to me in parting 'Empty *everything!*', which indeed is both excellent and classic.

'Everything is empty' means that every thing is *not there as such.* Any other interpretation is just misleading and *wrong.*

'Emptiness' is just overboard with everything.

Conceptualisation conceals what we are.
That is why mind must 'fast'.

❖   ❖   ❖

'Forgetfulness of the Self (omitting to remember This-which-I-am) is the source of all misery.' (Ramana Maharshi).

❖   ❖   ❖

Love-hate can have no existence outside the dualistic universe of sense-perception and personal experience. 'Impersonal love' is like 'immaterial matter', or any other contradiction in terms.

❖   ❖   ❖

There are divers absences. There is absence of every sensorially perceptible object whose phenomenal presence is the noumenal absence of Me. And there is the absence of my personal phenomenal presence, which is of what I personally appear to be: that absence is coexistent and coextensive with my phenomenal appearance. And there is the absence which I am, whose presence is whatever is sensorially perceptible to me.

But Absolute Absence is the source of all presence.

❖   ❖   ❖

When I am absent there is no Time, and it is always the present.

❖   ❖   ❖

'I am the presence of the absence of all that seems to be.' *(§ 37. Essential Definition)*

❖   ❖   ❖

One must recognise oneself as one's absence as subject.

Colophon

Ultimate Insight

> *There has never been an objective 'being'.*

That is the only absolute truth there could ever be. Why? Because from that alone can perfect understanding arise. Nor is any other apprehension needed, for all comprehension lies therein.

The perfect understanding of that is perfect understanding itself. And that is because only non-objectivity itself can know it.

There is nothing more to be said, and—ultimately— nothing but that need ever have been said.

> *'Knowing that, the rest is known.'* (An Upanishad)

TECHNICAL TERMS

There is probably no single cause of mis-understanding so general or so potent as the mistranslation of the word 'prajnā' as 'wisdom'.

Terminology

I

To CHOOSE conventional terms just because they are familiar is pandering to conditioning, whereas the only service we can render in publishing such a book as this is to break down that which is the supreme obstacle to understanding, which, precisely, is *conditioning*.

The Masters found it necessary to change their terminology and phraseology frequently in order to prevent the minds of their monks becoming conditioned and so attached to concepts which would have nullified their teaching. Our task is lighter: we merely need abandon inaccurate terms in favour of more correct ones.

II

Semantically Speaking

WORDS ARE too important to be abandoned to those who misuse them. In the absence of living Masters, the words of those no longer alive must serve in their stead. If people are confused or misled by them, the Masters are betrayed and what they taught is trailed in the mud.

Every technical term is a jewel, an intaglio to be closely examined, studied, and its detailed implications profoundly explored, for in those implications lie the secret heart of what the Masters were telling us. Interpreted in any sense other than that they intended, the words of their teaching are wasted, and we, their pupils, are turned away from their truth.

The meaning of words should be respected as profoundly as their speaker, and the exactitude of their meaning, rooted in their origin and their associations, never dissociated from their inseparable counterparts, should be meticulously preserved and scrupulously manipulated.

III

Zen

Zen in English is an Anglo-Nipponic term which seeks to attribute to a school of Japanese Buddhism the transmission of *Ch'an* which in China represented The Supreme Vehicle *(Shresthyāna)*. When used of contemporary Buddhism it can only apply to Japanese or Anglo-American developments of Ch'an: when used of the T'ang dynasty Buddhism in China it is misapplied for it did not yet exist: when used of contemporary Buddhism in China it is nonsense. There could be such a thing as 'Japanese Ch'an': there has never been, and is not, such a thing as 'Chinese Zen'.

The fact that the word *Zen* is the Japanese pronunciation of the Chinese word *Ch'an* which itself is the Chinese pronunciation of the Sanscrit word *Dhyāna*, should not imply that what has been made of Ch'an in Japan is what Ch'an either was or is in China, nor does either term mean what 'Dhyana' meant in India.

Far-reaching confusion and general misunderstanding has resulted from identifying the titles of these Sects with the etymological meaning of the Sanscrit word from which these sectarian titles derive.

They recognise the same Indian Sutras, and the Japanese recognise the ancient Chinese Masters, much as modern Christian denominations recognise the Pentateuch and the Judaic Prophets, but Ch'an remains Ch'an, and Zen is the interesting Japanese religion which the Japanese, in seven or eight centuries, have made of Ch'an.

IV

Advice

IN READING translations from the Chinese Masters: whenever you meet the term *The Way*—retranslate it and read it as *Tao;* whenever you meet the term *Wisdom*—retranslate it and read it as *Prajnā;* whenever you meet the term *Meditation*—retranslate it and read it as *Dhyāna.*[1] If you do this you will eventually, and perhaps rapidly, apprehend what the text is trying to convey to you: if you do not you may never know what these texts are seeking to reveal and, if you do, it will be after long months, and more probably many years wasted in the bye-paths of misunderstanding.

These are not the only terms to which this advice applies: it applies to all those for which no counterpart exists in our languages, but if you will follow it for these you will have occasion to rejoice.

[1] Other words than *Dhyāna* are mistranslated as 'meditation', but they never mean what 'meditation' etymologically implies: sometimes they mean 'sitting', which implies 'emptying' the mind of objects or allowing mind to 'fast'.

Tao

There is no 'Way', for a way implies someone to follow it and, as long as there is such a one, it can lead nowhere.

The use of the term demonstrates failure to understand.

A 'way' leads from here to there: from here to here there can be no 'way'.

V

Why Dhyāna and Prajnā are not Two

'FUNCTIONING' IS non-functioning or immutability subjected to the seriality of a time-context.

Functioning being an aspect of seriality, dependent on sequential duration, it seems evident that Prajnā, the functioning aspect of Dhyāna, is in fact Dhyāna, cognised as Prajnā, apparently functioning as a result of being interpreted subject to the sequence of time. Dhyāna, as the static aspect of Prajnā, remains intemporally as such, and 'Prajnā' is neither different nor separate from Dhyāna.

This seems clearly to demonstrate the Masters' statement concerning the indivisability of Dhyāna and Prajnā.

'Dhyāna', functional as Prajnā, is revealed as a symbol of what we are, both noumenally and phenomenally. Asked what Prajnā was, did not the Great Pearl answer: 'What could there be that is not Prajnā'? Phenomenally all we are is called Prajnā, noumenally all we are is called Dhyāna, and if they are neither separate nor different temporally and intemporally—nor are we, the presence or absence of a 'time' factor being an interpretive discrimination.

This surely applies to all aspects of phenomenality, and reveals them lucidly as what a Master such as Huang Po so clearly stated, i.e. that on no account must any distinction be imagined, for apperceiving them as inseparable is how a Buddha sees and so is buddhahood. In short—difference is apparent only, and is due to the sequential vision which we call 'time' and which constitutes the dualistic mechanism of subject perceiving object.

Note: It is only the apparent sequence of 'duration' which causes an apparent difference between noumenon and phenomena, between what is noumenal and what is phenomenal. This of course, refers to apperception by whole mind; dualistically conceived, as counterparts, they are apparently different indeed.

Bewildering Bits and Painful Pieces. VI

'*Meditation*'? If you mean what it says—don't do it! If you don't mean what it says—don't say it!

❖   ❖   ❖

Definition of Ch'an: Buddhism de-bunked and de-buddha'd.

❖   ❖   ❖

Basic Buddhism

Anyone who *practises* any form of Buddhism is surely a dubious Buddhist, and anyone who *practises* Ch'an cannot be a Ch'anist at all.

❖   ❖   ❖

'Words are the fog one has to see through'.

(D. E. HARDING)

❖   ❖   ❖

Ch'an is analytical
Vedanta is synthetic.

❖   ❖   ❖

Ch'an

If you think you are right
you are necessarily wrong.
If you think you are wrong
you are necessarily right.

❖   ❖   ❖

The Correct Use of Words

'The wrong identification of one thing with another is the work of the contaminated mind.' MAHARSHI, *Self-Inquiry*, page 21.

❖   ❖   ❖

Vedanta

Than 'That' does the dictionary hold a more unfortunate word to describe 'This-which-we-are'?

The negating of objects is at the same time the negating of their subject; negating of other than self is also the negating of self. All negating, therefore, is self-negating, and all positive affirmation is self-affirmation.

To use the word 'Real' is applying a phenomenal concept to noumenon; it is seeking to objectivise noumenality. Can we hope to find freedom from phenomenal bondage by such casuistry?

❖   ❖   ❖

It's not a holy mystery at all! It's a huge joke!

When the devout Emperor of China heard of Bodhidharma he sent for him and asked 'What is the essence of the Holy Buddhist Doctrine?'

'Majesty', replied Bodhidharma, 'there is no doctrine —and nothing holy about it whatever!'

Index

See also Contents. References are to the numbered sections. Certain terms such as noumenon and phenomena, subject and object, self and other, etc. which occur very frequently in the text will not be found in the Index. The aim of this Index is to enable readers to find a chapter in which they remember some technical term or other feature.

Sentient Publications, LLC publishes books on cultural creativity, experimental education, transformative spirituality, holistic health, new science, ecology, and other topics, approached from an integral viewpoint. Our authors are intensely interested in exploring the nature of life from fresh perspectives, addressing life's great questions, and fostering the full expression of the human potential. Sentient Publications' books arise from the spirit of inquiry and the richness of the inherent dialogue between writer and reader.

Our Culture Tools series is designed to give social catalyzers and cultural entrepreneurs the essential information, technology, and inspiration to forge a sustainable, creative, and compassionate world.

We are very interested in hearing from our readers. To direct suggestions or comments to us, or to be added to our mailing list, please contact:

SENTIENT PUBLICATIONS, LLC
1113 Spruce Street
Boulder, CO 80302
303-443-2188
contact@sentientpublications.com
www.sentientpublications.com